500 BROOCHES

500 BROOCHES
Inspiring Adornments for the Body

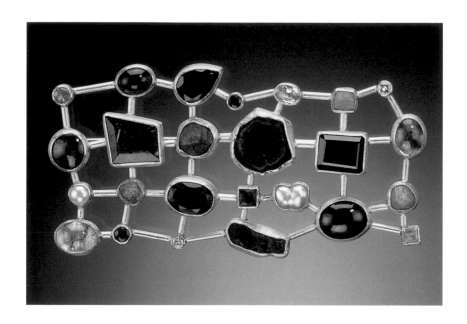

LARK BOOKS

A Division of Sterling Publishing Co., Inc.
New York

Editor: Marthe Le Van

Art Director: Dana Irwin

Cover Designer: Barbara Zaretsky

Assistant Editor: Nathalie Mornu

Assistant Art Director: Lance Wille

Editorial Assistance: Delores Gosnell,
Rosemary Kast, Jeff Hamilton

Editorial Interns: Amanda Wheeler,
Meghan McGuire, Janna Norton,
Matthew M. Paden

Proofreader: Sherry Hames

Cover:
JACQUELINE RYAN
Brooch, 2000

Spine:
ROBERTA AND DAVID WILLIAMSON
I Am Never Alone in My Garden, 2001

Back cover, top:
NANCY MICHEL
Journey Through the Underworld
(detail), 2003

Back cover, bottom right:
YEONMI KANG
I Waited for It All Day, 2003

Back cover, bottom left:
BILLIE JEAN THEIDE
Black and White Ruin, 2003

Front flap:
LISA AND SCOTT CYLINDER
Pencilated Woodpecker Brooch, 2004

Back flap:
HEATHER WHITE
Protean Cameo #7,
Protean Cameo #12, 2000

Title Page:
PETRA CLASS
Mosaic in Reds and Yellows, 2003

Opposite:
KAYO SAITO
Floating Brooch, 2001

Library of Congress Cataloging-in-Publication Data

500 brooches : inspiring adornments for the body / editor, Marthe Le Van ;
introduction by Marjorie Simon.
    p. cm.
 Includes index.
 ISBN 1-57990-612-5 (pbk.)
1. Jewelry making. 2. Brooches. I. Title: Five hundred brooches. II.
Le Van, Marthe.
TT212.A14 2005
391.7--dc22

2004014379

10 9 8 7 6 5 4

Published by Lark Books, A Division of
Sterling Publishing Co., Inc.
387 Park Avenue South, New York, N.Y. 10016

Distributed in Canada by Sterling Publishing,
c/o Canadian Manda Group, 165 Dufferin Street
Toronto, Ontario, Canada M6K 3H6

Distributed in the U.K. by Guild of Master Craftsman Publications Ltd., Castle Place,
166 High Street, Lewes, East Sussex, England BN7 1XU

Distributed in Australia by Capricorn Link (Australia) Pty Ltd.,
P.O. Box 704, Windsor, NSW 2756 Australia

If you have questions or comments about this book, please contact:
Lark Books
67 Broadway
Asheville, NC 28801
(828) 253-0467

Manufactured in China

ISBN 13: 978-1-57990-612-2
ISBN 10: 1-57990-612-5

For information about custom editions, special sales, premium and corporate
purchases, please contact Sterling Special Sales Department at 800-805-5489
or specialsales@sterlingpub.com.

CONTENTS

TODD REED
AMORPHIC DIAMOND CLUSTER #1, 2003

ALESSIA SEMERARO
JAZZ BAND #2, 2002

GIOVANNI CORVAJA
BROOCH, 2000

INTRODUCTION

It's a good bet that the first humans to wear clothes soon thought of pinning the garments together. Brooches, simple and noble, have adorned the clothing of men and women ever since. They have been both formal and narrative, spare and ornate, made of diamonds, iron, or diamonds and iron—probably every technique and material ever embraced by jewelers.

A thousand or more years ago, when pins held cloaks or togas together, the decorative *brooch* was more ornamental than the merely functional *pin*. Today we hardly distinguish between pins and brooches, except to elevate a pin by calling it a brooch. In cold climates such as Scandinavia and the mountains of central Asia, brooches evolved into large and elaborate objects representing the wearer's personal wealth.

Historical techniques, materials, and ancient themes keep coming back, or perhaps they never left. Roman soldiers arriving in the British Isles found Celtic warriors using champlevé enamel. Etruscan gold granulation disappeared for centuries, to reappear in the Renaissance. Carved gemstones, chasing and repoussé, ancient methods of creating a rich relief in metal using punches front and back, and lost-wax casting, known in Egypt and Africa, are still part of the jeweler's vocabulary. The cameo pin, Victorian hatpin, Chinese hairpin, Saxon ring brooch or gold circle pin, the Roman fibula, Anglo-Saxon, Viking, or Celtic disk brooch—all are remembered in this collection of 500 remarkable brooches.

What's new is the kind of commentary or narrative that characterizes the post-modern sensibility. Of course, in jewelry making it's not new to borrow or to copy motifs and themes. What seems a sign of the times is the kind of conscious reference to the *idea* of jewelry, specifically, the *idea* of the brooch. Some of the selected artists have taken a very straightforward, even conventional approach to adornment, while others have taken a leap to explore the boundaries of "broochness." There are moments of grace and flights of humor. Some artists may seem to go too far, others not quite far enough. Some are shocking in their subject matter, others in their elegance or simplicity, still others in their technical virtuosity.

Every age has its emblems and themes. Since the 1960s the use of so-called "alternative" materials has resulted in an irreverent and often playful art form. Such entries serve as markers of a given time, for they do not always maintain their pungency over time. Yet they stand as reminders of what was on people's minds, a snapshot of the times. The current

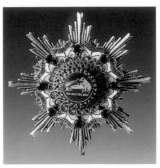

political theater is always evident, and this year was no exception. There were references to war and lots of Masonic and scouting badges. Personal, political, or social narrative brought the body image to the body. Jung-Hoo Kim's standing figures are contemplative, while Keith Lewis' chased and repoussé diver is more confrontational.

Enamel is enjoying a nice ascendancy at the moment, and in nontraditional ways. Backing off from fussy cloisonné, people are experimenting with throwing a skin of glass on a metal form. Surfaces range from a satiny finish hand-stoned under water to an under-fired, rough, "sugar" texture. Color made a big appearance, not only with enamel and gemstones, as is traditional, but with painted and lacquered wood, pigmented resin, balloons, plastic tags, fabric, paper, and of course, the ubiquitous found object. Sally Marsland made a strong statement using just black and white. And just when you think nothing new could be said with an aluminum soda can, Karin Seufert's cross adds another voice.

Though it seems obvious to say it, a jeweler's primary referent is the human body. We choose the brooch format because

WEARABILITY IS, TO PARAPHRASE MOZART, THE OBEDIENT HANDMAIDEN OF THE IDEA.

it is like a tiny canvas where ideas may be expressed. When I make a brooch I'm thinking about pinning it on a piece of clothing, not resting on skin, as a necklace might be. Like all jewelry design, weight and wearability are primary considerations. Occasionally, however, the concept takes over and wearability is, to paraphrase Mozart, the obedient handmaiden of the idea. In this international selection the viewer will see both concept and wearability. The *idea* of the brooch will occasionally take precedence over the actual brooch. Two good examples are Cathelijne Engelkes' stamps depicting the percentage of major elements present in the human body, and Monika Brugger's shirt, thread, and pin in a box. They have what I call "essential broochness," an object quality that distinguishes them from necklaces or rings.

Looking over the many submissions, I was reminded of how much creativity may be unleashed by setting limits. It is always thrilling to see an artist reach for the big idea, regardless of whether it can be pinned on a good black dress.

Marjorie Simon

PIERRE CAVALAN
VICTORIA CROSS MEDAL FOR A NEW DAY, 2002–2003

JUNG-HOO KIM
THE OX GAME, 1997

MONIKA BRUGGER
SEWN WITH RED THREAD, 2003

*M*y inspiration to use enamel in my work is a result of my desire to represent the essence of natural history images that intrigue me. I use colored enamels to adorn the metal as others might use gemstones. The color palate, variations, and combinations that are available to me with this media offer an endless supply to satisfy my method of expression.

— DAVID C. FREDA

DAVID C. FREDA

FIREBIRD, 2003

8.3 X 2.5 X 2.5 CM

24-KARAT YELLOW GOLD, 18-KARAT YELLOW GOLD, 14-KARAT YELLOW GOLD, FINE SILVER, ENAMEL, PEARL; HOLLOW-CORE CAST, HAMMER TEXTURED, GRANULATED

Photo by Erica and Harold Van Pelt

Collection of Susan Beech

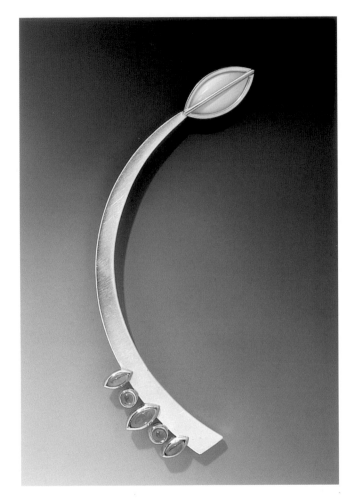

JANIS KERMAN

BROOCH, 2002

11.4 x 1.9 CM

STERLING SILVER, 18-KARAT GOLD, MOTHER-OF-PEARL, PERIDOT

Photo by artist

HEATHER WHITE

STUDY OF IMPERFECTION #4, 2002

6.4 X 2.5 X 1.3 CM

18-KARAT GOLD, ETTRINGITE;

LOST WAX CAST, FABRICATED

Photo by Dean Powell

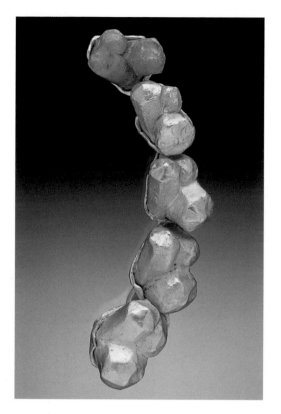

The series of brooches entitled Study of Imperfection *makes use of mapping. I begin each piece with a colored gemstone or mineral in the rough. I then observe the crystalline structure of each to create mirroring shapes in wax that I cast into gold. The stones and minerals appear as they are found in nature, wonderfully flawed. So it is the material of value, the gold, that traces the shape of each imperfect gemstone. By assembling all of the pieces together, the result is a journey of observation, the stone or mineral as the guide to unconventional beauty.*

— HEATHER WHITE

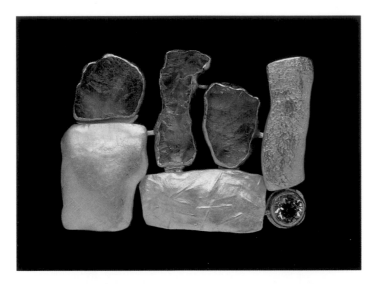

NANCY MICHEL

UNTITLED, 2002

5.1 X 3.8 X 0.8 CM

AQUAMARINE CRYSTALS, SAPPHIRE,
18-KARAT GOLD, 22-KARAT GOLD,
24-KARAT GOLD;
CONSTRUCTED, REPOUSSÉ

Photo by Dean Powell

SEUNG-HEA LEE

BROOCHES, 2001

LEFT, 6.2 X 4.8 X 1 CM;
RIGHT, 4.8 X 4.8 X 1 CM

SILVER, 18-KARAT GOLD;
FOLDED, FABRICATED

Photo by Mark Johnston

LISA GRALNICK

THREE BROOCHES, 2002

1.9 X 7 TO 8.3 CM IN DIAMETER

18-KARAT GOLD; FABRICATED

Photo by artist

*O*ver the past several years, I have completed a group of brooches in thin-gauge gold sheet by employing a direct method of fabrication reminiscent of the paper models that are often precursors to works in metal. The pieces examine structure as I understand it in music—as a closed and rigid system that implodes from within, capable of disintegrating into a distinct temporality that is at once an irreproducible expressive phenomenon and a rational mathematical proof. — LISA GRALNICK

CASTELLO HANSEN

UNTITLED, 2003

4.7 X 4.7 X 2.2 CM

CIBATOOL®, GOLD LEAF, LACQUER, 18-KARAT GOLD, SILVER;
TURNED, PRESSED, FORGED, SOLDERED, PAINTED, OXIDIZED

Photo by artist

MARCIA A. MACDONALD

LEFT TO RIGHT: *USE THE INTERNAL ANTENNAE, STAND UP FOR WHAT YOU BELIEVE IN, HOLLOW VICTORIES*, 2003
EACH, 17.8 X 3.8 X 1.6 CM
WOOD, PAINT, STERLING SILVER, EGGSHELL, THERMOPLASTIC, MICA; CARVED
Photo by Hap Sakwa

FELIEKE VAN DER LEEST

THE GREY LADY WITH THE CHICKEN LEGS, 2004

9.5 X 5.5 X 2.5 CM

TEXTILE, RUBBER, HEMATITE, STORE-BOUGHT TOY;

CROCHETED, KNITTED

Photo by Eddo Hartmann

BARBARA SEIDENATH

SULPHUR, 2001

4 X 3.7 X 0.6 CM

ENAMEL, STERLING SILVER

Photo by Marty Doyle

Courtesy of Sienna Gallery,

Lenox Massachusetts

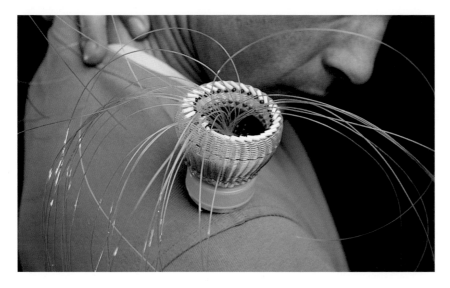

SHELLEY NORTON

UNTITLED, 2001

15 X 10 X 10 CM

MONOFILAMENT, BEADS, SEQUINS, PLASTIC
BOTTLE TOP, STERLING SILVER; WOVEN

Photo by John Collie

CYNTHIA TOOPS

MOSS, 2004

3.2 X 10.8 X 1.3 CM

POLYMER CLAY, STEEL

Photo by Roger Schreiber

I have been using polymer clay threads in my
micro-mosaic work for many years, and
decided to experiment with embedding it vertically
instead of horizontally. — CYNTHIA TOOPS

BRIDGET CATCHPOLE

PRICKLE, 2002

1.9 X 8.3 X 1.3 CM

STERLING SILVER, SYNTHETIC BRISTLES; CONSTRUCTED

Photo by Anthony McLean

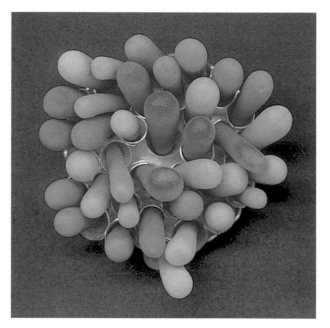

SUSAN KASSON SLOAN

PINK BROOCH, 2002

11.4 X 6.4 X 3.2 CM

EPOXY RESIN, PIGMENTS

Photo by Ralph Gabriner

REBECCA HANNON

ANEMONE PIN, 2003

3.8 X 3.8 X 3.2 CM

SILVER, PLASTIC; FABRICATED, RIVETED

Photo by artist

VICKI MASON

CIRCUMCHROMA, 2003

3.8 x 3.8 x 1.8 CM

PVC SHEET, STERLING SILVER; DYED, COILED

Photo by Grant Hancock

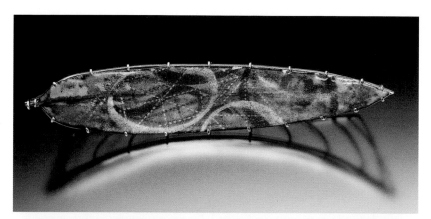

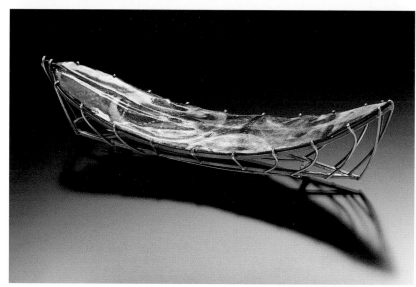

NANCY BONNEMA

BAMBOO BROOCH, 2003

3.8 X 2.5 X 15.2 CM

ENAMEL, COPPER,

STERLING SILVER;

RISO SCREENED

Photos by Doug Yaple

ELEANOR MOTY

OPAL BROOCH, 2002

8.3 x 2.2 x 0.6 CM

STERLING SILVER, 22-KARAT GOLD,

18-KARAT GOLD, PEARL STEM, OPAL,

LABRADORITE; FABRICATED

Photo by artist

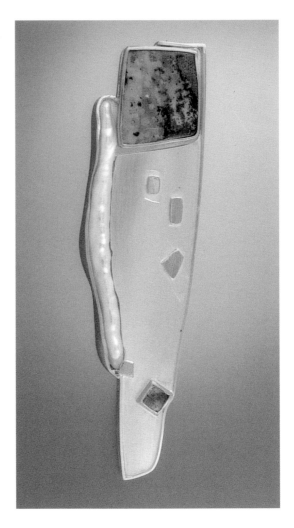

My work reflects a quiet still life against the backdrop of the dramatic splash of fire emanating from the blacksmith's sledgehammer hitting red-hot steel. — NAMU CHO

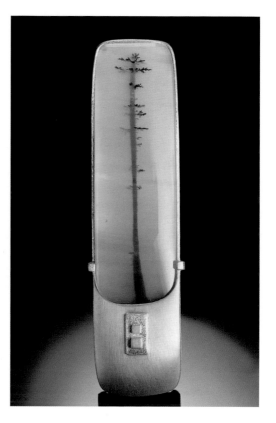

LILLY FITZGERALD

PIN, 2000

7.6 X 1.9 CM

22-KARAT GOLD, AGATE; HAND-FABRICATED

Photo by artist

NAMU CHO

MIRAGE 3-2, 2004

8.9 X 3.2 CM

DAMASCENE, 22-KARAT GOLD, DIAMONDS

Photo by Hap Sakwa

SCOTT CORMIER

THE TRAVELER #2, 2002

4.4 X 7.6 X 0.1 CM

18-KARAT RED GOLD, LUCITE, OIL PAINT;

SCORED, FILED, SOLDERED

Photo by David Witbeck

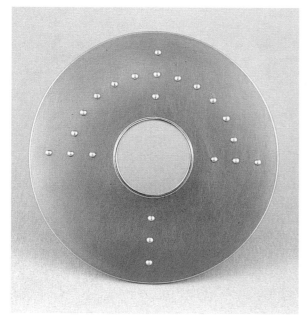 

ABRASHA

HARD DISK BROOCH WITH BEZEL, 1993

0.9 x 6.5 CM IN DIAMETER

RECYCLED ALUMINUM HARD-DISK PLATTER, STERLING SILVER, 18-KARAT

GOLD, 24-KARAT GOLD, STAINLESS STEEL; FABRICATED, RIVETED

Photos by artist

MYOUNG SUN LEE

PSYCHOLOGICAL DISTANCE 2, 2003

6 X 6 X 0.5 CM

SILVER

Photos by Myung-Wook Huh (Studio Munch)

DOROTHY HOGG MBE

RED CIRCLE BROOCH WHICH CASTS A SHADOW, 2000

1.5 X 10 CM IN DIAMETER

STERLING SILVER, 18-KARAT GOLD, FELT; OXIDIZED

Photo by Shannon Tofts

Collection of National Museums of Scotland

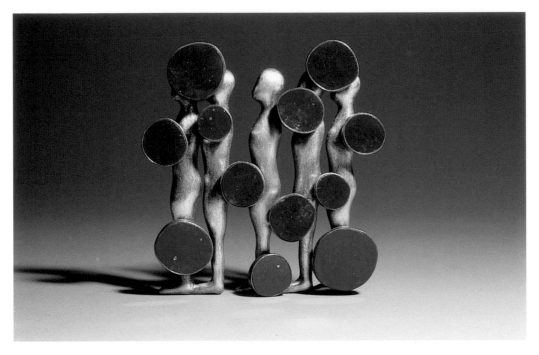

JUNG-HOO KIM

THE DROPS, 2003

6.4 X 7.6 X 1.9 CM

STERLING SILVER, LAPIS LAZULI

Photo by In-Shik Kim

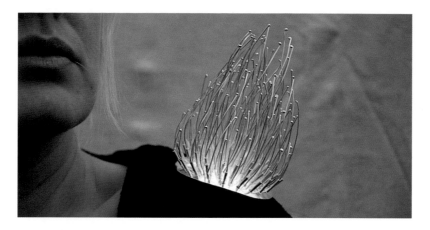

ÅSA HALLDIN

DANDELION DEW, 2002

10 x 6 CM

SILVER; SOLDERED

Photo by Adrian Nordenborg

JULIE BLYFIELD

PRESSED LEAF AND SHADOW BROOCH SERIES, 2003

VARIOUS DIMENSIONS

STERLING SILVER; CHASED

Photo by Grant Hancock

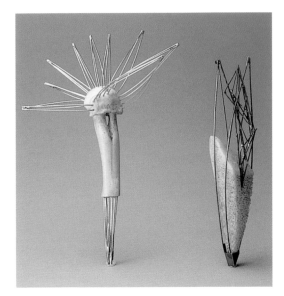

WOOK KOH

EXTINCTION, 2002

LARGEST, 11 X 7 X 2 CM

BONE, STAINLESS STEEL, IRON, STERLING SILVER

Photos by Myung-Wook Huh (Studio Munch)

BIBA SCHUTZ

MEMORIES, 2000

4.4 X 7.6 X 1.3 CM

STERLING SILVER; CONSTRUCTED, OXIDIZED

Photo by Ron Boszko

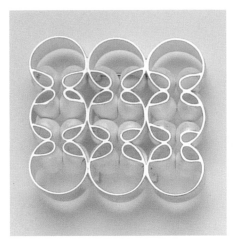

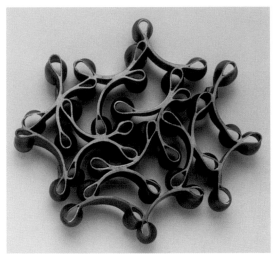

SABINE STEINHÄUSLER

SCHLAUFENBROSCHEN (LOOP BROOCHES), 2003

LEFT, 3.7 X 4.1 X 1.3 CM; RIGHT, 6 X 7 X 1.1 CM

SILVER; OXIDIZED

Photos by Paul Müller

JAN YAGER

DANDELION BROOCH, 2001

12.7 x 12.7 x 0.6 CM

STERLING SILVER, AUTO GLASS

Photo by Jack Ramsdale

JOHN IVERSEN

LEAF PINS, 2000

AVERAGE, 10.2 x 6.4 x 0.1 CM

18-KARAT GOLD, STERLING SILVER;

CARVED, CAST, CONSTRUCTED, OXIDIZED

Photo by Kenji-Ishii

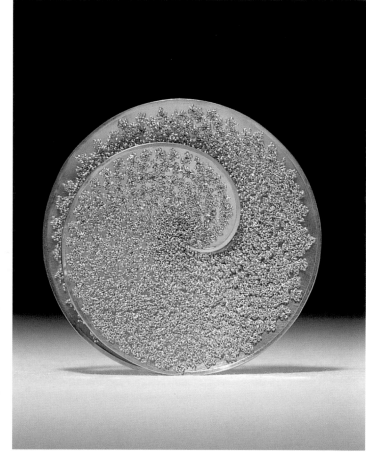

GIOVANNI CORVAJA

BROOCH, 2000

6 x 6 x 1 CM

PLATINUM, FINE GOLD; GRANULATED

Photos by artist

BELINDA NEWICK

A KIN (DETAIL), 2004

6.4 X 5.4 X 2 CM

FINE SILVER, STERLING SILVER; FLY-PRESS FORMED,

COMPUTER-ENGRAVED HANDWRITING

Photo by Grant Hancock

GREGORÉ MORIN

KING OF THE SEA, 2000

8.5 X 4.5 X 1 CM

YELLOW SAPPHIRE, GARNETS, PEARLS, DIAMOND,

BLACK JADE, GOLD; HAND-FABRICATED

Photo by John Parrish

CARMEN AMADOR

LA BUSQUEDA (THE SEARCH), 2000

5.5 X 6.7 X 1.5 CM

SILVER, GOLD; CHASED, REPOUSSÉ

Photo by artist

REINA MIA BRILL

ODELIA, 2004

38.1 x 15.2 x 7.6 CM

EPOXY RESIN, WIRE, NICKEL;

MACHINE-KNITTED

Photo by artist

BRAD BARTLETT

MONKEY SEE, MONKEY DO, 1998

12 x 3.2 x 2.8 CM

STERLING SILVER, BRASS, BRONZE,

24-KARAT GOLD LEAF, SYNTHETIC RUBIES;

FABRICATED, CAST

Photo by artist

SARA WASHBUSH

MR. SUSPICIOUS, 2002

6.4 x 3.8 x 1.6 CM

ALLOY, STERLING SILVER,

GESSO, COLORED PENCIL;

CHASED, REPOUSSÉ, FABRICATED

Photo by artist

BERIT TEEÄÄR

ROSY, 2002

4 x 5 x 7 CM

LATEX, WOOD, SILVER, GLASS BEADS; BEADED

Photo by Mihkel Valdma

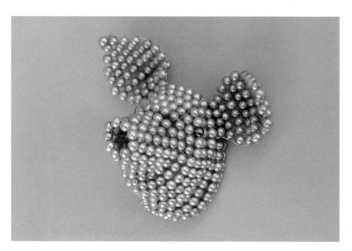

DAVID BIELANDER

PEARL PIG, 2003

7 x 7 x 7 CM

FRESHWATER PEARLS, 18-KARAT GOLD

Photo by artist

NATHANIEL DELARGE

2-13-03, 2003

8.9 x 5.7 x 5 CM

COPPER, PLASTIC DEER

Photo by Don Brazil

KELLY BUNTIN JOHNSON

NUESTRA SEÑORA DE GUADALUPE

(OUR LADY OF GUADALUPE), 1999

10.2 X 6.4 X 0.6 CM

EUROPEAN GLASS SEED BEADS, LEATHER, MEDAL;

EMBROIDERED

Photo by artist

MARY FRISBEE JOHNSON

MEDAL FOR EXPLORATION, 2003

12 X 5.1 X 1.3 CM

STERLING SILVER, FOUND VINTAGE

LITHOGRAPHED TIN, FOUND STERLING

SILVER CHARM, AMETHYST,

MEDAL RIBBON, NICKEL SILVER;

FABRICATED, RIVETED, ETCHED

Photo by artist

KEVIN GLENN CRANE

HAVE YOU SEEN THE ELEPHANT?, 2002

4.5 X 2.1 X 2 CM

18-KARAT YELLOW GOLD, STERLING

SILVER, MABE PEARL, MASTODON FOSSIL,

NATURAL DIAMOND, MOTHER-OF-PEARL,

BRIOLETTE-CUT SAPPHIRE

Photo by Doug Yaple

T he Badge *is a humorously critical brooch inspired by* The Patriot Act. *It's a very fake badge trying quite hard to look real. In its already tarnished copper,* The Badge *reveals the flaws of the act.*

— KEN THIBADO

KEN THIBADO

THE BADGE, 2003

6.4 X 6.4 X 1.3 CM

DIAMONDS, 14-KARAT GOLD, STERLING SILVER, COPPER, BRASS, FOUND OBJECTS; SOLDERED, COLD CONNECTED

Photo by Robert Diamante

GISBERT STACH

PIN UP, 1998

9.5 X 4.5 X 0.5 CM

ALUMINUM SIGN, CONDOM, SAFETY PIN; FOLDED, SAWED, RIVETED

Photo by artist

CATHELIJNE ENGELKES

PLATED POSTCARD CITIES, 2002

BROOCHES, 2 X 1 CM; DISPLAY, 12.2 X 16.5 X 3.5 CM

POSTCARDS, BOX, SILVER, GOLD; PLATED

Photo by Ted Noten

A special piece of the postcard is copied to scale and formed into a silver or gold brooch. The brooches are attached to the postcard fitting into the image and presented as a wearable souvenir.

— CATHELIJNE ENGELKES

REBECCA A. STRZELEC

WRITTEN BROOCH, 2003

13.1 x 11.4 x 11.9 CM

RAPID PROTOTYPE ABS PLASTIC,

MEDICAL ADHESIVE

Photo by Adam Vorlicek

The relationship between my brooches and the body is one of an echo. Through form-language and material choice, I reiterate the shape and surface of bone, muscle, and ligament. I wish to communicate a growth or an appendage that has developed from beneath the skin. While drawing inspiration from the female body, it is my intention to create hybrid organic forms that resist direct identification. Eliminating the traditional need of clothing as the attaching surface, I ask the viewer/wearer to see the brooch in the context of the naked female form. When worn, a dramatic tension is created as brooches are placed immediately on the skin, adhering and adapting to the surfaces of the body.

— REBECCA A. STRZELEC

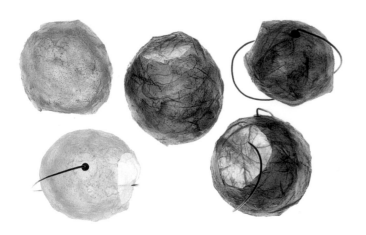

These egg-shaped brooches were inspired by femininity, fertility…fragility, strength.

— YOKO SHIMIZU

YOKO SHIMIZU

EGGS, 2003

EACH, 5 X 4 X 4 CM

PAPER, RESIN, SILVER

Photo by Federico Cavacchioli

MARZIA ROSSI

ICE, 2002

7 X 6.5 X 0.9 CM

THERMOPLASTIC, SILVER, GLASS

Photo by Federico Cavicchioli

SVENJA JOHN

ANILLO BROOCH, 2001

3.5 x 12 CM IN DIAMETER

POLYCARBONATE; SURFACE TREATED,

CONSTRUCTED, COLORED

Photo by Jörg Fahlenkamp

SHANNON CARNEY

RESIN RINGS BROOCH, 2003

9.1 x 8.4 x 0.4 CM

RESIN, STERLING SILVER

Photo by Anya Pinchuk

KARIN SEUFERT

UNTITLED, 1999

EACH, 3.5 X 3.5 X 4 CM

FOIL, SILVER

Photo by artist

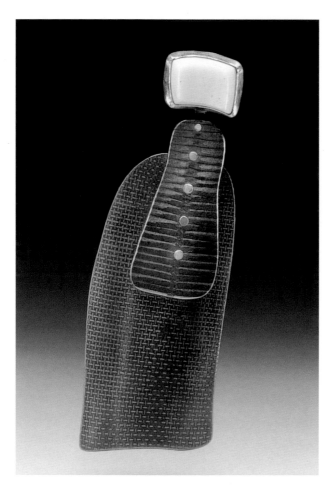

BROOKE BATTLES

WOMEN I'VE KNOWN #4, 1998

10.2 X 3.5 X 1.3 CM

STERLING SILVER, BRASS, COPPER,

FINE SILVER, 14-KARAT GOLD, BONE;

FABRICATED, FUSED

Photo by Hap Sakwa

M*y work reflects my fascination with the unending nuance of nature's wildness. My unmanicured textures, my dense, dark finishes, my irregular stones and forms all give my work the sense of the organic, the suggestion of age and experience.*

— BROOKE BATTLES

GRAZIANO VISINTIN

UNTITLED, 1997

9 X 1.5 CM

18-KARAT GOLD; NIELLO

Photo by Lorenzo Trento

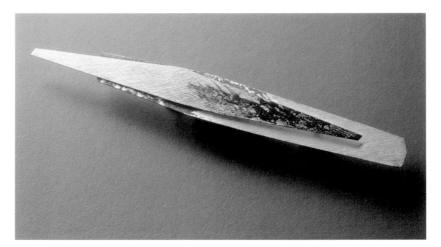

ELEANOR MOTY

ARROYO, 2000

10.2 X 2.5 X 1 CM

STERLING SILVER, 18-KARAT GOLD,

RUTILATED QUARTZ, SAPPHIRE;

FABRICATED

Photo by artist

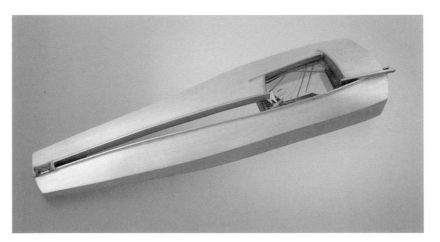

HEE-SEUNG KOH

COLLECTED OBJECTS, 2003

6.7 X 8 X 1.5 CM

STERLING SILVER, PAPER, BAMBOO, LAPIS LAZULI,

IRONSTONE, IVORY

Photo by Kwang-Choon Park

PETER HOOGEBOOM

PERSONAL FLOWER II, 1997

LEFT, 4.5 X 3.5 X 1.5 CM;

CENTER, 8 X 3 X 1 CM;

RIGHT, 6 X 3.5 X 1.5 CM

PORCELAIN, SILVER, STEEL

Photo by Hennie van Beek

HYUNG-LAN CHOI

ASSOCIATION, 2002

LEFT, 4.5 X 6.5 X 2 CM;

CENTER, 4.2 X 8.5 X 2 CM;

RIGHT, 4.5 X 6.2 X 2 CM

SILVER, IVORY, IRON, PAPER

Photo by Myung-Wook Huh

(Studio Munch)

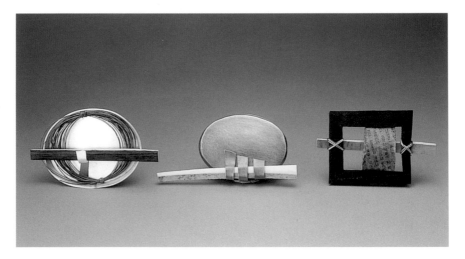

SHANA KROIZ

TIN CAN SERIES, 2001–2002

7.6 X 1.3 CM

TIN CANS, PEARLS, BEZEL WIRE, ACETATE;

DIE FORMED, RIVETED, CARVED

Photo by Edwin Seidel

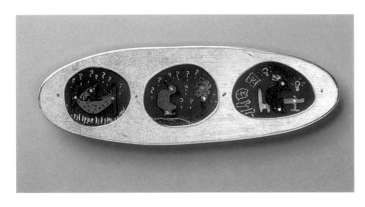

In my latest works, one can detect a certain influence from Pop Art. These brooches, consisting of small pictures executed in various shades of titanium, tell small stories like in a cartoon strip.
— JEANETTE LOPEZ-ZEPEDA

JEANETTE LOPEZ-ZEPEDA

IDEA POPS UP!, 2003

4 X 9 X 0.5 CM

SILVER, GOLD LEAF, TITANIUM; KNITTED

Photo by Ole Akhøj

ANDREA WIPPERMANN

SCHWEINE IN DER STADT, 2004

3 X 7 CM

GOLD, CORAL; CAST

Photo by Helga Schulze-Brinkop

STEPHANIE JENDIS

MALLORCA, 2003

7.5 X 16 X 1 CM

SYNTHETIC RESIN, FIBERGLASS,

SYNTHETIC STONES, SILVER

Photo by Ron Zijlstra

I found the piece of synthetic resin on a beach on the Spanish island of Mallorca. I think it was part of a boat or a surfboard; now it's the base of a new story.

— STEPHANIE JENDIS

CHRISTOPHER A. HENTZ

GOLDEN AURA BROOCH, 2002

7.6 x 7.6 x 1.3 CM

18-KARAT GOLD, SILVER,

BLUE SPINEL, WHITE SAPPHIRE;

CHASED, FORMED, FABRICATED

Photo by Ralph Gabriner

JENNIFER TRASK

POPILLIA JAPONICA, 2001

3.2 x 2.4 x 0.6 CM

18-KARAT GOLD, 22-KARAT GOLD,

JAPANESE BEETLES, MINERAL CRYSTAL

Photo by Dean Powell

ANDY COOPERMAN

ROYAL JELLY, 2000

4.4 CM WIDE

BRONZE, STERLING SILVER, 18-KARAT GOLD,
PEARLS, DIAMOND; FABRICATED

Photo by Douglas Yaple

I remember as a boy opening an Edmund Scientific catalog to the page featuring paramecium cultures. The text described an entire world—invisible to the unaided eye—whirling away in a single drop of cloudy pond water. The notion that a complex and dense universe, poignant and complete, could exist, unseen and literally at my fingertips, galvanized my curiosity. What else had I misunderstood, overlooked, or dismissed as simple? My view of the world shifted. And it's through this lens that I most enjoy peering.

The visual vocabulary that I choose is grounded in science. It relies on the combination and juxtaposition of industrial and naturally occurring forms such as accreted skins and rivets, or strapped and braced skeletal forms, to create metaphors for growth, decay, and repair. These metaphors, I believe, offer insight into the wider and deeper issues that confront, confound, and excite us throughout our lives. People should discover more about one of my pieces each time they pick it up.

— ANDY COOPERMAN

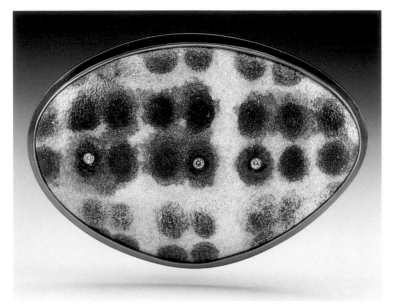

APRIL HIGASHI

UNTITLED, 2004

4.4 x 6.4 x 1 CM

ENAMEL, DIAMONDS, 18-KARAT GOLD,

22-KARAT GOLD, SILVER

Photo by Hap Sakwa

CARMEN AMADOR

LA RUEDA DE LA FORTUNA

(THE WHEEL OF FORTUNE), 2002

2 x 5.5 CM IN DIAMETER

SILVER, NICKEL SILVER,

GOLD, RUBY; SOLDERED

Photo by artist

DIANE FALKENHAGEN

HEAVENLY BLUE MORNING GLORY, 2001

2.5 X 7.6 CM IN DIAMETER

STERLING SILVER, POLYMER CLAY;

FABRICATED, TRANSFERRED IMAGE

Photos by Chris Arend

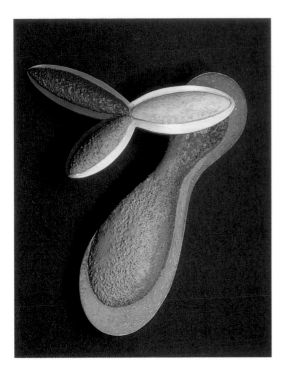

SUZANNE ESSER

UNTITLED, 2003

6.5 X 4.5 X 2 CM

SILVER, SAND, PAINT; SOLDERED

Photo by Ron Zijlstra

JEFFREY LLOYD DEVER

LUSH, 2003

6.4 X 3.8 X 1.3 CM

POLYMER CLAY;

HOLLOW-FORM CONSTRUCTED, CARVED, DRILLED

Photo by Gregory B. Staley

KATHLEEN BROWNE

SECRETLY SHE WISHED SHE COULD..., 1999

8.9 x 8.9 x 0.6 CM

STERLING SILVER, COPPER,

ENAMEL DECAL; FABRICATED

Photo by artist

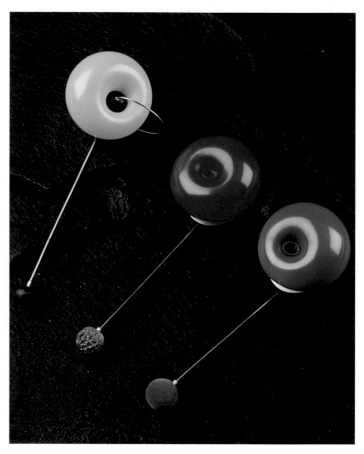

SUNGHO CHO

PRESS THE BALLOON, 1998

EACH, 15 X 5 X 2.5 CM

BALLOON, MAGNET, WOOD, STAINLESS STEEL

Photo by Hong-gu Shim

PATRICK MARCHAL

GIVE ME FIGHT, 2002

9 X 9 X 1.2 CM

STAINLESS STEEL, SILVER, LACQUER, COLOR TRANSFER;

DIGITALLY MILLED, POLISHED, CUT, FITTED,

SOLDERED, RIVETED, SURFACE TREATED

Photo by P. Louis

Most of my pieces tell a story. The story is simplified into a single symbolic object, or a symbolic combination of materials and imagery. The dichotomies of life intrigue me most—the way our most divine impulses coexist with our most earth-bound ones, or the way our most serious moments also have an aspect of humor, if you can just step back from them. That's why you'll find contrasting materials and images in my work, like precious metals alongside rusted steel, or sterling silver cast in forms of brittle-looking twigs and branches.

— MARCIA A. MACDONALD

MARCIA A. MACDONALD

BLACK & YELLOW POLKA DOTTED TUTU BROOCH, 2002

11.4 x 5.1 x 2.5 CM

WOOD, PAINT, STERLING SILVER, 14-KARAT GOLD, EGGSHELL, GLASS; CARVED, FABRICATED

Photo by Hap Sakwa

ROBERTA AND DAVID WILLIAMSON

I LONG FOR YOUR TOUCH, 2001

9.5 x 6.4 x 1.3 CM

STERLING SILVER, QUARTZ CRYSTAL, SHELL,

ABALONE, BRASS, ANTIQUE LITHOGRAPH;

FABRICATED, FORMED, SOLDERED

Photo by James Beards

JAN SMITH

POPPY BROOCH (WITH CUSTOM TRAVEL BOX), 2003

BROOCH, 5.1 X 0.3 CM; BOX, 10.2 X 10.2 X 2.5 CM

DOUGLAS FIR, MICA, STERLING SILVER, POPPY POD, COPPER,

ENAMEL, 22-KARAT GOLD BIMETAL; RISO SCREENED

Photo by Doug Yaple

LINDA MACNEIL

ROYAL WATERS, 2003

11.4 X 5.1 X 1.9 CM

GLASS, 24-KARAT GOLD,

BRASS, 14-KARAT GOLD;

ACID POLISHED, PLATED

Photo by Bill Truslow

JULIA TURNER

UNTITLED, 2004

4.4 X 5 X 0.6 CM

EBONY PANEL, 18-KARAT GOLD,

22-KARAT GOLD;

FACETED, FABRICATED

Photo by artist

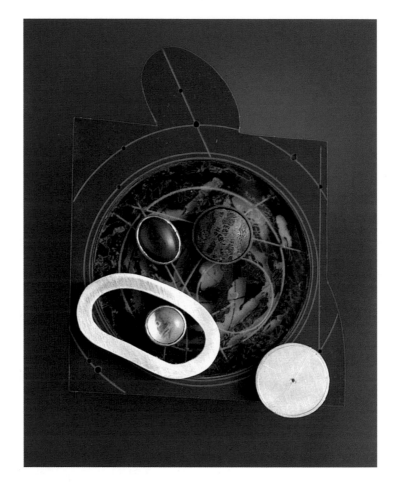

RAMON PUIG CUYÀS

RED BIRD, 2002

6 X 5 X 1 CM

SILVER, WOOD, PLASTIC, QUARTZ,

PAPER, CORAL; ASSEMBLED

Photo by artist

E*lvira,*

The everblue varicose veins
are the price of her evergreen hips

And the long neck
of the giraffe helps her

Curious look

also to view into
the well-hidden heart.
— SILVIA WALZ

SILVIA WALZ

ELVIRA, 2003

8.5 x 2.5 x 0.3 CM

SILVER, COPPER, CORAL,

PLASTIC, PHOTOGRAPH

Photo by Ramon Puig Cuyàs

JOSÉE DESJARDINS

CLÉOME ASARUM, FROM THE SERIES

HERBARIUM REVISITED, 1996

6 x 1.6 CM

STERLING SILVER, 14-KARAT GOLD,

ENAMEL, STAUROLITE; LOST WAX CAST

Photo by artist

SANDRA NOBLE GOSS

BIG BAY BEACH MEMORIES, 2000

25.4 X 20.3 CM

STERLING SILVER, BRONZE, BRASS, COPPER, PHOTOGRAPH,

STONE, MAP, ACRYLIC, PATINA; MARRIED METAL, ETCHED

Photo by Jeremy Jones

RANDY LONG

ST. LUCY, 2001

4.1 X 5.7 X 1.6 CM

SHELL CAMEO, 22-KARAT GOLD; CARVED

Photo by artist

I fell in love with the sensuous qualities of a large shell cameo I purchased in Italy, and decided I wanted to teach myself to carve shell cameos. I did not know of any art jewelers using this ancient technique in their work, so I thought this would provide an opportunity to express something unique in our field. I decided to carve shell cameos of saints because of a renewed interest in my faith and my desire to work with images that I have admired in Italian paintings of the 13th and 14th centuries.

— RANDY LONG

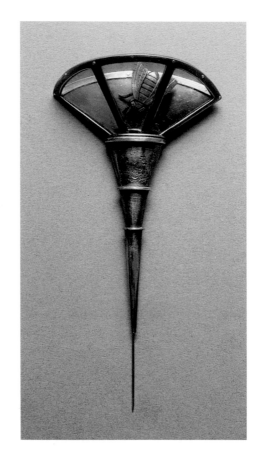

KIFF SLEMMONS

SCONCE, 2001

10.2 x 6.4 x 1.9 CM

STERLING SILVER, BRASS, MICA;

FABRICATED

Photo by Rod Slemmons

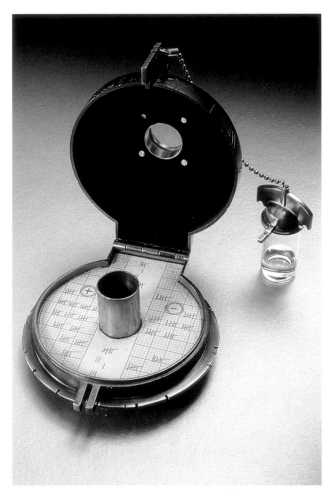

KRISTIN MITSU SHIGA

TEARS WON'T HELP BROOCH, 2001

7.6 X 5.7 X 5 CM

COPPER, STERLING SILVER, BRASS, GLASS,

STEEL, TEARS, CHARTING PAPER;

HYDRAULIC-PRESS FABRICATED, ETCHED

Photos by Courtney Frisse

REIKO ISHIYAMA

No. 2, 2003

7 x 7 x 1.9 CM

18-KARAT GOLD, STERLING SILVER; MARRIED METAL,

PIERCED, HAMMERED, SHAPED, OXIDIZED

Photo by Dean Powell

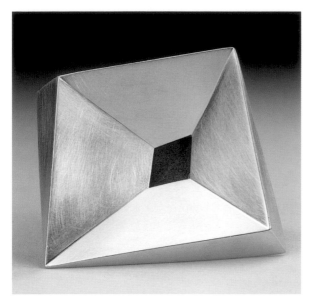

SEUNG HYE CHOI

OUT THE WINDOW, 2003

4.5 X 5 X 1 CM

18-KARAT GOLD, ENAMEL;
SET, SCORED

Photo by Mark Johnston

MUNYA AVIGAIL UPIN

HOMAGE TO LEGER, 1977

5 X 7.6 X 1.3 CM

STERLING SILVER, COPPER,
THERMOPLASTIC; FABRICATED

Photo by artist

CATHY CHOTARD

UNTITLED, 2003

5.8 X 4.2 X 0.8 CM

SILVER

Photo by artist

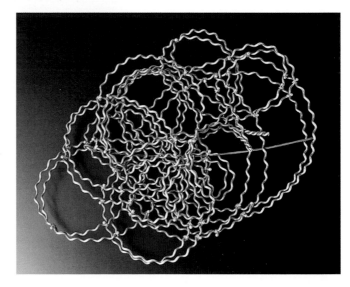

SUSAN CROSS

CRIMP #1, 2003

13 X 9 CM

SILVER, 18-KARAT GOLD; OXIDIZED

Photo by Joël Degen

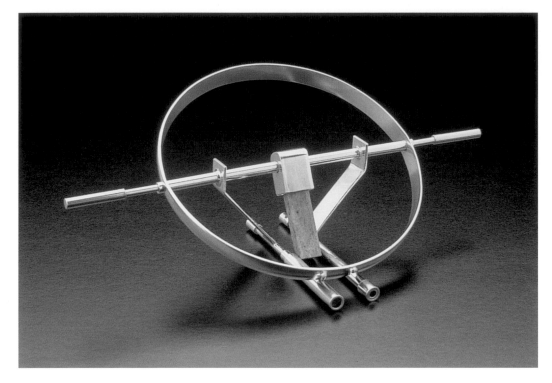

HARLEY McDANIEL

NATIVE CRUCIFIX BROOCH, 1999

10.2 x 7.6 x 10.2 CM

STERLING SILVER, COPPER, BEAD; FABRICATED

Photo by Keith Meiser

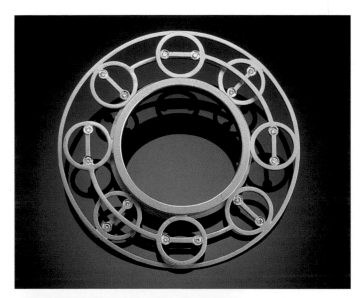

*V*isually, my work alludes to structures and objects we have created as a species. Emphasizing construction and surface, I strive to showcase the underlying forms of architectural elements, clockworks, and machine parts. Making these pieces completely by hand with the bare minimum of hand tools causes me to continually think about the role of the craftsman within our technologically driven society.

— GEOFFREY D. GILES

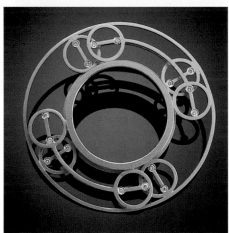

GEOFFREY D. GILES

ROTATIONAL SERIES #3, 2002

5.4 X 5.4 X 1 CM

18-KARAT YELLOW GOLD,

14-KARAT WHITE GOLD, DIAMONDS;

FABRICATED, SOLDERED

Photos by Taylor Dabney

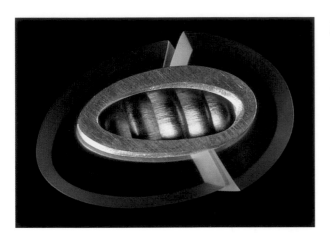

KAREN McCREARY

Chiton Brooch, 2003

5.7 x 7.6 x 1 cm

ACRYLIC, ALUMINUM, STERLING SILVER,

22-KARAT GOLD LEAF;

CARVED, FABRICATED

Photo by artist

JUNG HEE SHIN

A Motif Made From Young Rak, 2000

6.7 x 0.8 cm

Photo by Kwang-Choon Park

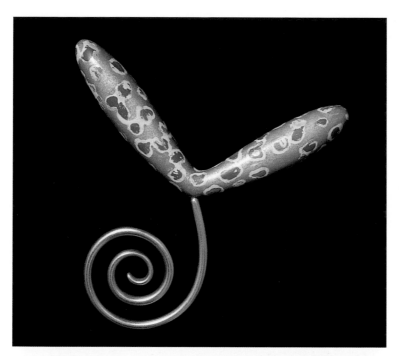

BRUCE METCALF

SPROING, 2003

8.9 X 8.9 CM

MAPLE, BRASS, GOLD; CARVED,

PAINTED, FORGED, PLATED

Photo by artist

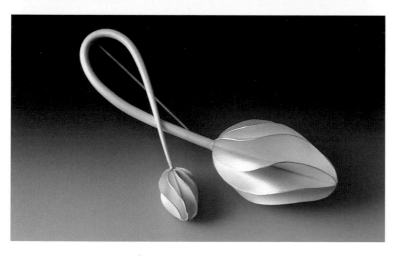

CHIH-WEN CHIU

BUD I, 2001

10.2 X 5.1 X 2.5 CM

FINE SILVER, STERLING SILVER;

HAMMERED, SOLDERED

Photo by Dan Neuberger

DORIS MANINGER

NOTHING A ROUND, 2003

3 x 5 x 0.5 CM

22-KARAT GOLD, PIECE OF 18TH CENTURY WATCH,

RUBY; CONSTRUCTED

Photo by Federico Cavicchioli

MARTINA MÜHLFELLNER

UNTITLED, 2001

5 X 7.5 X 1 CM

STERLING SILVER, ENAMEL;

CAST, CONSTRUCTED

Photo by Federico Cavicchioli

JUNG-HOO KIM

THE CHAIR, 1998

6 X 8.5 X 1.9 CM

STERLING SILVER, SLATE,

24-KARAT GOLD; KUM BOO

Photo by In-Shik Kim

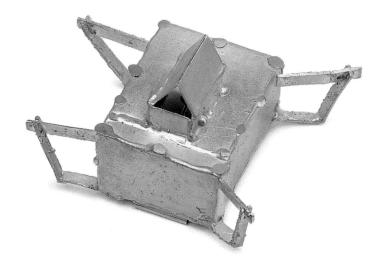

ANDREA WIPPERMANN

ATICO, 2003

2.5 x 4.5 x 3.5 CM

GOLD; CAST

Photo by Helga Schulze-Brinkop

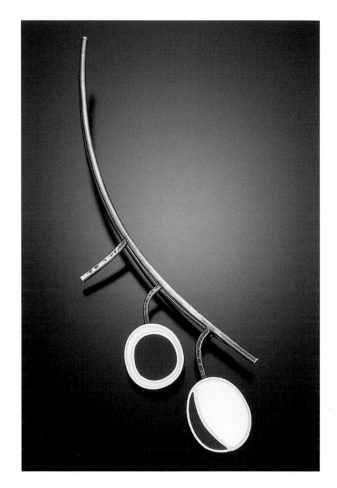

SADIE WANG

FRUIT BROOCH, 2002

13.3 x 4.4 x 0.6 CM

STERLING SILVER, EPOXY RESIN; OXIDIZED

Photo by azadphoto.com

YU-CHUN CHEN

UNTITLED, 2002

3.7 X 4.2 X 0.6 CM

STERLING SILVER, COPPER, ENAMEL

Photo by Federico Cavicchioli

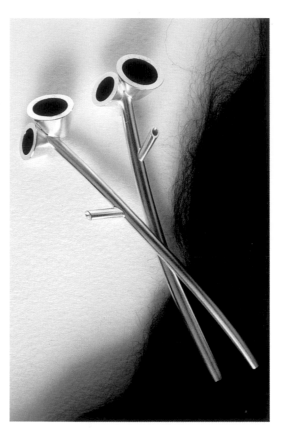

DOROTHY HOGG MBE

BROOCH IN THE ARTERY SERIES, 2003

10 X 5.5 X 1.2 CM

SILVER, FELT

Photo by John K. McGregor

85

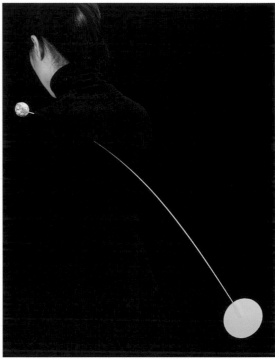

SEOYOUN CHOI

MOBILE 3, 2001

EACH, 75 X 15 X 1 CM

SILVER, STAINLESS STEEL, FILM

Photo by Myung-Wook Huh (Studio Munch)

SEOYOUN CHOI

MOBILE 1, 2001

80 X 10 X 30 CM

MIXED MEDIA

Photo by Myung-Wook Huh (Studio Munch)

BORIS BALLY

NICKEL GRABBER BROOCHES, 2000

EACH, 7 x 7 x 1.3 CM

RECYCLED ALUMINUM BUS PLACARD, LICENSE PLATE;

HAND-FABRICATED, PRESS FORMED, RIVETED

Photo by Dean Powell

JANTJE FLEISCHHUT

AMETHYST, 2002

3 X 4 X 9 CM

FIBERGLASS, SILVER; CONSTRUCTED

Photos by Eddo Hartmann

DAPHNE KRINOS

BROOCH MY ENGLAND, 2003

6 X 5 X 0.7 CM

SILVER, AMETHYSTS; OXIDIZED

Photo by Joël Degen

SUSAN CROSS

CHROMA, 2003

5 X 5 CM

SILVER, BEADING ELASTIC; OXIDIZED

Photo by Joël Degen

REBECCA HANNON

ROOFTOPS BROOCH, 2003

5.1 X 6.4 X 0.6 CM

SILVER, GOLD, PHOTOGRAPH;

SOLDERED, CUT, REASSEMBLED

Photos by artist

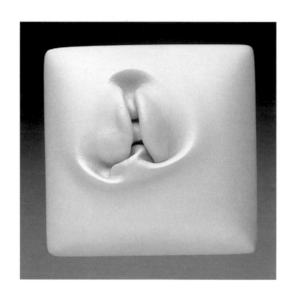

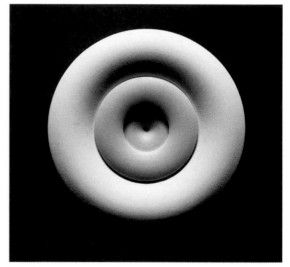

YUYEN CHANG

UNTITLED BROOCH IN THE *ORIFICE SERIES*, 2002

5.1 X 5.1 X 1.9 CM

SILVER

Photo by Jim Wildeman

CASTELLO HANSEN

UNTITLED, 2003

4.6 X 4.6 X 7.5 CM

CIBATOOL®, RECONSTRUCTED CORAL, SILVER, PAINT;

TURNED, PRESSED, SOLDERED

Photo by artist

SEUNG HYE CHOI

SPRING SNOW, 2002

5.3 x 5.3 x 7 CM

STERLING SILVER, ENAMEL

Photo by Studio Munch

93

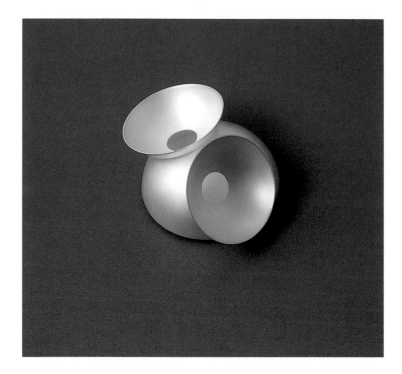

THERESE HILBERT

VESSEL, 2003

3.8 X 7.3 X 5.4 CM

SILVER

Photo by Otto Künzli

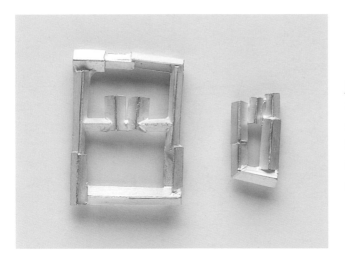

SILKE TREKEL

BROOCHES STADTLANDSCHAFTEN
(BROOCHES CITY LANDSCAPES), 2001

LEFT, 6.5 X 4 X 1 CM

SILVER; CAST

Photo by Helga Schulze-Brinkop

OLIVER FUETING

WATCH ME, 2002

4 X 6 CM IN DIAMETER

STERLING SILVER, STEEL, PAINT

Photo by Federico Cavicchioli

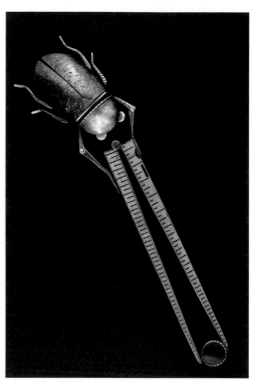

LINDA DARTY

GARDEN BROOCHES: AUTUMN, 2003

EACH, 10.2 X 1.3 X 0.6 CM

COPPER, ENAMEL, STERLING SILVER,

FINE SILVER, GEMSTONES;

FABRICATED, LIMOGES ENAMELED

Photo by artist

KIFF SLEMMONS

TWEEZE, 2003

14 X 4.4 X 0.5 CM

STERLING SILVER, COPPER,

WOOD RULER; FABRICATED

Photo by Rod Slemmons

YEONMI KANG

I Waited for It All Day, 2003

7.5 x 7.8 x 2.5 cm

STERLING SILVER, WOOD, 24-KARAT GOLD LEAF;

CAST, FABRICATED, PAINTED, KUM BOO

Photo by Yongwha Kang

NANCY MICHEL

JOURNEY THROUGH THE UNDERWORLD, 2003

4.8 x 7.6 x 1.1 CM

MEXICAN OPAL BEADS, TURQUOISE BEADS,
18-KARAT GOLD, 22-KARAT GOLD,
24-KARAT GOLD, IVORY, SILVER,
GOLD LEAF, EPOXY; HAND-FABRICATED,
SWEDGED, FORMED, CAST

Photos by Dean Powell

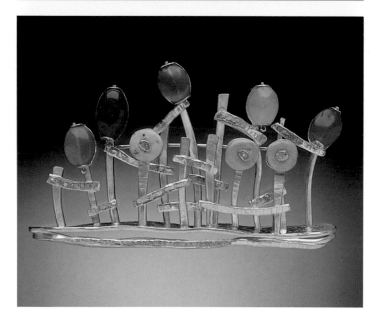

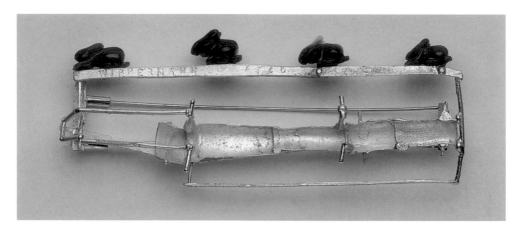

A N D R E A W I P P E R M A N N

H A S E N I N D E R S T A D T, 2003

3 x 7.5 CM

GOLD, CORAL; CAST

Photo by Christof Sandig

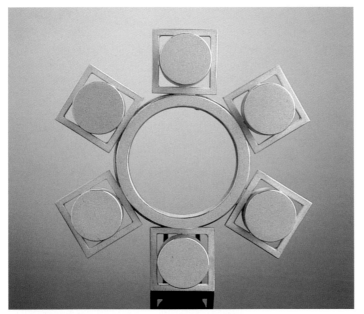

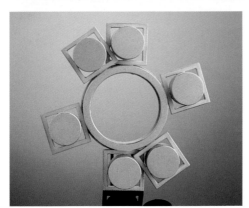

GEOFFREY D. GILES

ROTATIONAL SERIES #7, 2003

5.1 x 5.1 x 1.3 CM

18-KARAT YELLOW GOLD,

14-KARAT WHITE GOLD;

FABRICATED, HOLLOW FORMED,

SOLDERED

Photos by Taylor Dabney

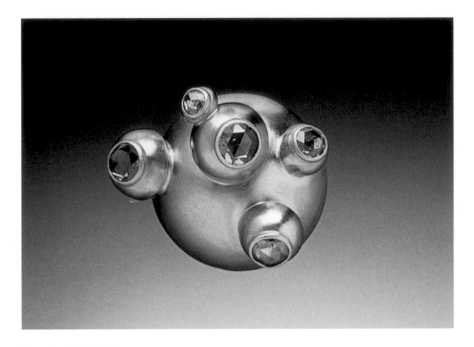

LOLA BROOKS

BROOCH, 2002

1.6 X 2 X 1.5 CM

STAINLESS STEEL, CHAMPAGNE ROSE-CUT DIAMONDS, 18-KARAT GOLD;

HOLLOW CONSTRUCTED, SOLDERED

Photo by Dean Powell

MARTINA MÜHLFELLNER

ON THE STEP, 2002

9 X 6.5 X 1 CM

SILVER, ENAMEL; CONSTRUCTED

Photo by Federico Cavicchioli

KIM SO-YOUNG

HIS SILENCE, 2003

5.7 X 4.5 X 2.5 CM

PAPER, STERLING SILVER, COPPER

Photo by Myung-Wook Huh (Studio Munch)

KARRIE HARBART

UNTITLED, 2004

22 X 3 X 1 CM

ALABASTER, WHEAT STAMEN,

STERLING SILVER, EPOXY; CARVED

Photo by artist

DEBORAH LOZIER

ACCORDION BROOCH/DOUBLE VS, 2002

1.6 X 8.9 X 1.3 CM

ENAMEL, COPPER; FOLDED, PIERCED,

WELDED, SOLDERED, TORCH FIRED

Photo by artist

RAMON PUIG CUYÀS

RELIQUARY, 2003

8.5 X 4.5 X 1.1 CM

SILVER, NICKEL SILVER, WOOD,

PLASTIC, FOUND OBJECTS;

ASSEMBLED

Photo by artist

SILKE TREKEL

BROOCHES DÄCHER (BROOCHES ROOFS), 2001

ROUND, 2 X 7 CM IN DIAMETER

BALSA WOOD; LAMINATED, PAINTED

Photo by Helga Schulze-Brinkop

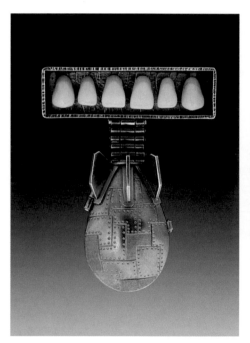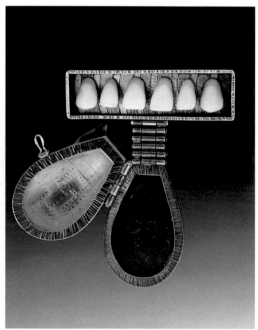

TIMOTHY LAZURE

OUT WITH DAD, 2003

4.8 x 6.4 x 1.1 CM

STERLING SILVER, COPPER, DENTAL SAMPLE

Photos by artist

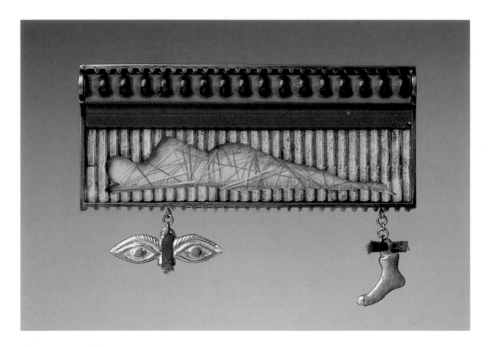

CYNTHIA CETLIN

SIESTA, 2003

6 x 9.1 x 0.6 CM

COPPER, WOOD, BRASS, PAPER, FIBERGLASS, RIBBON;

SOLDERED, PAINTED, COLD CONNECTED

Photo by Tim Thayer

MARCEL VAN KAN

18 CARAT BROOCH, 2002

4 X 6 X 0.5 CM

18-KARAT GOLD, BRASS, SAFETY
PINS; SOLDERED, PLATED

Photo by artist

With this brooch I wanted to represent the 18-karat gold alloy as a wearable trademark in fashion. It gives the person who wears it a number that's freely interpretable. At the same time, it can create distance because of the unemotional expression the brooch gives you.

— MARCEL VAN KAN

KIKKAN HULTHÉN

MINA HUNDAR (MY DOGS), 2001

LONGEST, 18 X 0.1 CM

IRON, LINSEED OIL; FIRED, SCRATCHED

Photo by artist

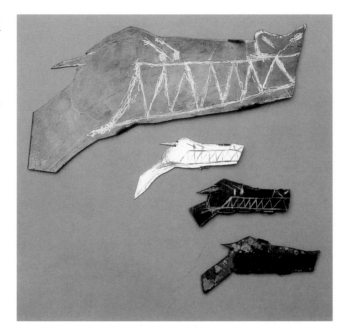

CRISTINA FILIPE

THING (FOR USE ATTACHED TO CLOTHING),
1991–2004

4 X 4 X 0.1 CM

IRON; ETCHED

Photo by SA Fotografias, Lda

*S*timulus and response. Attraction is my recent interest. How organisms lure others to meet their needs is as complicated as it is compelling. In my Lure Series, I have focused on the anatomy of floral forms to create creatures of allure. My hope is that the wearing of these brooches stimulates a response as provocative as the pieces themselves. — EDWARD L. MCCARTNEY

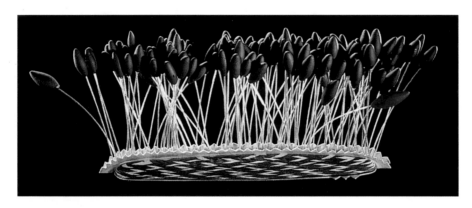

EDWARD L. MCCARTNEY

LURE SERIES, POTENTIAL EPAULET, 2003

17.8 x 2.5 x 7.6 CM

WOOD, STERLING SILVER, POLYMER CLAY,

STAINLESS STEEL; ANILINE DYED, LAMINATED

Photo by Jack B. Zilker

CATHERINE HILLS

PAPER, STONE & SCISSORS BROOCH, 2000

8 x 5 x 2 CM

SILVER, 18-KARAT YELLOW GOLD;

PRESSED, FABRICATED, CAST, OXIDIZED

Photo by Joël Degen

BIBA SCHUTZ

CUSHION, 2003

7.6 X 7.6 X 1.4 CM

COPPER, BRONZE, STERLING SILVER, FINE SILVER; CONSTRUCTED, FORGED, WRAPPED, OXIDIZED

Photo by Ron Boszko

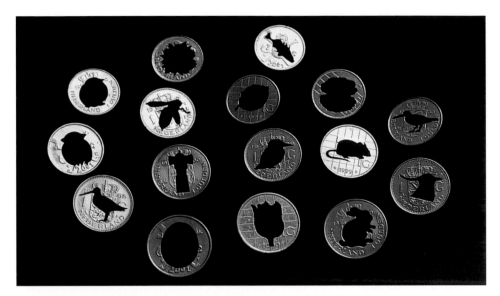

MARCEL VAN KAN

SILENT RESISTANCE, 2001

EACH, 0.2 X 2.4 CM

IN DIAMETER

NICKEL COINS,

SAFETY PINS; SOLDERED

Photos by Ted Noten

This brooch series explores identity. During the occupation of World War II, the Dutch people made jewelry out of the guilder, the country's currency, as an act of silent resistance that showed their respect and trust for their queen. — MARCEL VAN KAN

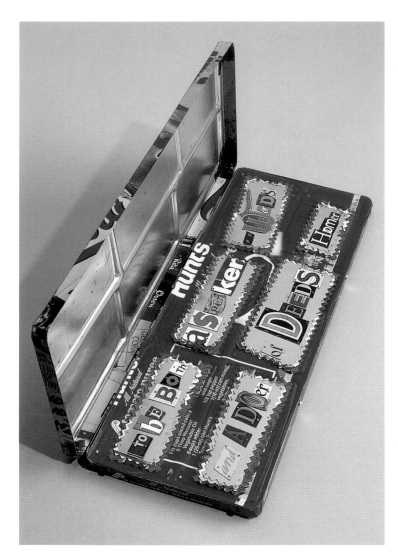

HARRIETE ESTEL BERMAN

TO BE BOTH, 1999–2004

1.6 X 30 X 12.7 CM

PRE-PRINTED STEEL,

10-KARAT GOLD, BRASS, STEEL;

PRESSED, RIVETED, SCREWED

Photo by Philip Cohen

My work is fabricated from post-consumer recycled tin containers. The re-use of discarded materials addresses a spectrum of social and political issues. The cultural values promoted by the marketplace—and ultimately found in our junk piles—provide fodder for ideas, insight, and inspiration. By reclaiming from the excesses of our consumer society, we renew hope for the future.

— HARRIETE ESTEL BERMAN

113

SARAH ENOCH

THREECOLOUR-BROOCHES (FIVE BROOCHES), 2003

EACH, 5.5 X 5.5 X 2.5 CM

POLYETHYLENE; THERMOFORMED

Photo by Tom Noz

MEGAN AUMAN

GARDEN PARTY, 2004

EACH, 20.3 X 7.6 X 7.6 CM

BALLOONS, STERLING SILVER, COPPER;

SEWN, FABRICATED

Photos by artist

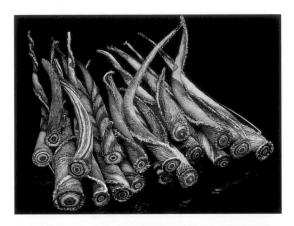

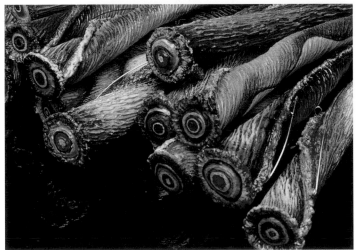

MARJORIE SCHICK

DE LA LUNA / DEL SOL, 1998–2004

LARGEST, 45.5 X 5 CM

CANVAS, STAINLESS STEEL PINS; STITCHED, STUFFED, PAINTED

Photos by Gary Pollmiller

LOUISE PERRONE

BOASTFUL, FROM *THE LANGUAGE OF FLOWERS* SERIES, 2001

18 X 17 X 5 CM

ALUMINUM, SILVER, IOLITE;

CHASED, ANODIZED

Photo by artist

MICHAL BAR-ON

BLACK WREATH #4, 2002

8.5 X 8.5 X 1 CM

SILVER, GOLD LEAF, ENAMEL;

SEWN, SOLDERED, CHAMPLEVÉ

Photo by Leonid Padrul

MARJORIE SIMON

Two Zinnias, 2003

7.6 TO 8.9 CM IN DIAMETER X 0.6 CM

STERLING SILVER, ENAMEL, COPPER;

DIE FORMED, PIERCED, FABRICATED

Photo by Ralph Gabriner

ROBERTA AND DAVID
WILLIAMSON

*I Am Never Alone
in My Garden*, 2001
10.8 x 7 x 1.9 cm
STERLING SILVER, ABALONE,
RUTILATED QUARTZ, PERIDOT,
WATCHMAKER'S CRYSTAL, BRASS,
ANTIQUE LITHOGRAPH, TIN;
FABRICATED, FORMED, SOLDERED
Photo by James Beards

YEONMI KANG

BLOOMING, 2003

7.2 X 4.8 X 2.5 CM

STERLING SILVER, ENAMEL, WOOD, 24-KARAT

GOLD LEAF; CAST, FABRICATED, KUM BOO

Photo by Yongwha Kang

TAWEESAK MOLSAWAT

TIME SERIES: ARTICLE NO. 4:

ADAM & ST-EVE, 2002

8.9 X 4.4 X 0.6 CM

STERLING SILVER, ENAMEL, COPPER,

LAZERTRAN®, DRIED APPLE PEEL,

HUMAN HAIR

Photo by artist

*M*y bugs were inspired by a trip my daughter and I took to Ecuador. We traveled up the Amazon Basin and stayed in a primitive cabin in the jungle, half a day's journey from power and civilization. We went to birdwatch, which was fantastic, but I left being most amazed by the bugs, bugs, bugs.
— NANCY DANIELS HUBERT

NANCY DANIELS HUBERT

BEETLE, 2001

8.3 x 8.9 CM

STERLING SILVER, MOUNTAIN AGATE, GLASS

TAXIDERMY EYES, TURQUOISE, FOSSIL

MAMMOTH IVORY, DRUZY, BLACK ONYX, TIN CAN

Photo by Jerry Anthony

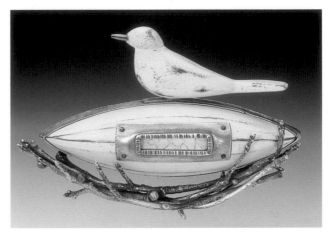

MARCIA A. MACDONALD

PEACE, 2003

7.6 X 11.4 X 2.5 CM

STERLING SILVER, WOOD, PAINT, EGGSHELL, THERMOPLASTIC

Photo by Hap Sakwa

KEN VICKERSON

TABLEAU VI—THOUGHT AND MEMORY, 1999

7 X 4.4 X 1.3 CM

STERLING SILVER, LABRADORITE, PINK PEARL;

FABRICATED, FUSED

Photo by Keith Betteridge

The title comes from Norse legend: two ravens, Hugin and Munin, perch on Odin's shoulder at sunset and whisper the news of Valhalla in his ear. The ravens pictured in the brooch playfully pass a stick between themselves, referring to the knowledge passed between generations. The pierced ravens reveal the labradorite set on the back panel of the brooch, which gives them a snow-blown look. The egg-shaped pearl pendant is an allusion to the passage of time.

— KEN VICKERSON

KAYO SAITO

FLOATING BROOCH, 2001

10 TO 12 X 10 CM IN DIAMETER

PAPER, POLYESTER FIBER, MAGNETS

Photos by artist

JULIE BLYFIELD

SLICED POD BROOCHES, 2003

EACH, 7.5 X 8.5 X 2.5 CM

STERLING SILVER; RAISED, CUT, CHASED

Photo by Grant Hancock

The pieces of reconstructed ivory push against each other and make a sound when the brooch is worn.
— STEPHANIE JENDIS

STEPHANIE JENDIS

UNTITLED, 2003

9 X 4 X 2.5 CM

RECONSTRUCTED IVORY,

CERAMIC, SILVER

Photo by Thomas Lenden

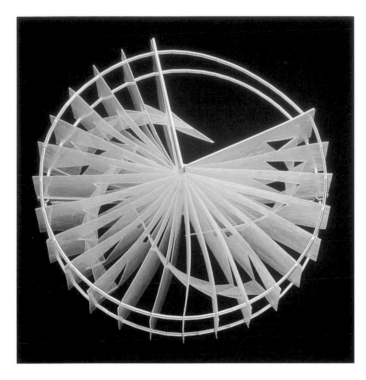

YUKA SAITO

NAMIKAZE, 2003

10 x 10 x 5 CM

STERLING SILVER, POLYPROPYLENE

Photo by Koji Akita

JOSÉE DESJARDINS

CAREX VERIS, FROM THE SERIES
HERBARIUM REVISITED, 1998

7.1 x 2.8 CM

STERLING SILVER, CHRYSOBERYL,
ENAMEL, VERMEIL; LOST WAX CAST

Photo by Pierre Fauteux

125

TRICIA LACHOWIEC

SNOWFLAKE FLORET, 2002

3.4 CM IN DIAMETER

STERLING SILVER; PIERCED

Photos by Dean Powell

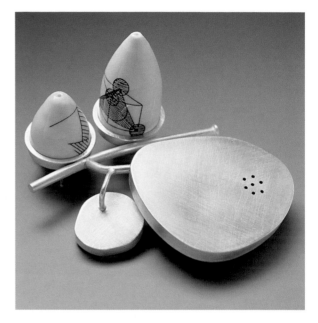

KATJA PRINS

UNTITLED, 2002

9 X 7 X 5 CM

SILVER, PORCELAIN

Photo by Eddo Hartmann

KYUNG-HEE KIM

DAYS OF EDEN—ADAM AND EVE, 2003

LARGEST, 6 X 5.5 X 0.7 CM

STERLING SILVER

Photos by Myung-Wook Huh (Studio Munch)

T. J. LECHTENBERG

OVAL BROOCH, 2003

4.4 X 8.3 X 2.5 CM

18-KARAT GOLD, 14-KARAT GOLD,
ACRYLIC; FABRICATED

Photos by artist

BARBARA SEIDENATH

NEST BROOCH, 2002

4.1 x 4.1 x 1.3 CM

ENAMEL, STERLING SILVER

Photo by Marty Doyle

Courtesy of Sienna Gallery,

Lenox, Massachusetts

CAROL-LYNN SWOL

UNTITLED, 2004

10.2 x 3.2 x 1.9 CM

STERLING SILVER, TYVEK®;

DYED, STACKED

Photo by artist

I look for inspiration in the natural world and in the material culture of our early human ancestors. I am fascinated with human cognitive growth and how that manifests in the objects we create.

I use the Tyvek®'s paper-like qualities and its inherent strength to work with the material in a manner in which paper cannot be used. It is in the duality of this material, which can look like pulp paper but can act so differently, that I yearn to find a sophisticated balance between intention and spontaneity.

— CAROL-LYNN SWOL

129

JANTJE FLEISCHHUT

PEDAL, 2002

5.5 X 3.5 X 4 CM

FIBERGLASS, SILVER; CONSTRUCTED

Photo by Eddo Hartmann

TRACEY CLEMENT

WINTER BROOCHES, 2001

EACH, 1 CM X 4 TO 6 CM IN DIAMETER

ENAMEL, MILD STEEL, STERLING SILVER

Photo by artist

DONALD FRIEDLICH

INTERFERENCE SERIES BROOCH, 2003

7 X 7 X 1.6 CM

WOOD, 14-KARAT GOLD, 18-KARAT GOLD,

22-KARAT GOLD; LATHE-TURNED, SANDBLASTED,

CONSTRUCTED, PAINTED

Photo by James Beards

ALESSIA SEMERARO

JAZZ BAND #2, 2002

4.5 X 8 X 1 CM

IRON, SILVER; PIERCED,
SOLDERED, RIVETED

Photo by Rayboom

JAMES OBERMEIER

SUBURBAN LANDSCAPE BROOCH #2, 2002

3.2 X 5 X 1.3 CM

SHIBUICHI, 24-KARAT GOLD, COPPER, PATINA;
POURED, CONSTRUCTED, COLORED

Photo by artist

TIM MCCREIGHT

BROOCH, 2001

5.7 CM IN DIAMETER

SILVER INGOT; FORGED, CHISEL CUT

Photo by Robert Diamante

Léola Le Blanc

Maudit Jésus Christ! I (Damned Jesus Christ! I), 2003

Each, 6 x 5 cm

Deer antler, core resin, sterling silver, copper, porcupine quills; burned, dyed

Photo by artist

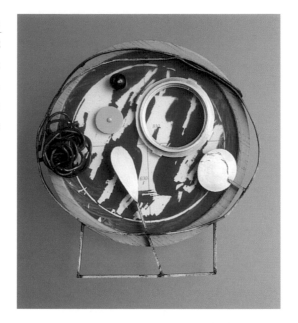

Ramon Puig Cuyàs

From to Be Born the Wind, 2002

6.5 x 7 x 1 cm

Silver, nickel silver, wood, plastic,
glass, paper, cornaline; assembled

Photo by artist

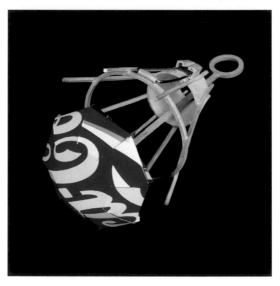

Karin Seufert

Colinoor, 1995

4 x 4 x 7 cm

Soda can, silver, remanium;
cut, slit, folded

Photo by Karen Bell

ERIN DOLMAN

SWEET RELEASE, 2003

3 X 5.5 X 1 CM

STERLING SILVER, 18-KARAT GOLD,
THERMOPLASTIC, FEATHER, SEAWEED,
TEXT FROM VINTAGE HYMN BOOK;
FABRICATED, CAST, RIVETED

Photo by artist

WIM VAN DOORSCHODT

WITH LOVE, 2003

6.5 X 13 X 1 CM

ACRYLIC; LAMINATED

Photo by Tom Noz

MARJORIE SIMON

SUNFLOWER SILHOUETTE, 2003

8.9 CM IN DIAMETER X 0.6 CM

STERLING SILVER, ENAMEL, IRON; CAST, FABRICATED

Photo by Robert Diamante

ROBERT W. EBENDORF

PASSION, 2003

1.3 X 6.4 CM IN DIAMETER

JAR LID, GLASS, IRON WIRE,

COPPER, POSTCARD

Photo by Bobby Hansson

JOHAN VAN ASWEGEN

LOOKING UP, 1999

4 X 3 X 1 CM

STERLING SILVER, ENAMEL

Photo by Mark Johnston

Courtesy of Sienna Gallery,

Lenox, Massachusetts

Representative of traditional mourning jewelry, this piece mirrors the cavities of the skull. Small silver tears hang and undulate from the edges.

— JOHAN VAN ASWEGEN

CHRIS IRICK

OVAL BROOCH SERIES I, 2003

LEFT, 5 X 2.5 X 1.3 CM

STERLING SILVER, MICA,

STAINLESS STEEL; FABRICATED

Photos by artist

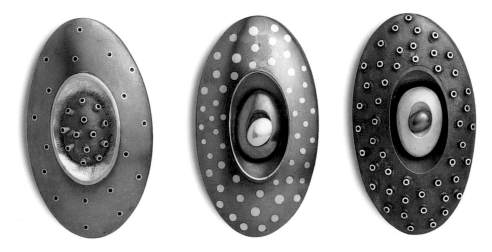

CATHERINE HILLS

SEE NO EVIL, HEAR NO EVIL, SPEAK NO EVIL BROOCHES FOR A WICKED WORLD, 1997

EACH, 6 X 3.5 X 2 CM

SILVER, 18-KARAT GOLD; PRESSED, FABRICATED, OXIDIZED

Photo by Tony May

Brooches are like poetry: personal observations, often subtle and emotional. They just float out there, surfacing on their own without the apparent constraints of wearability. Then, they become part of the wearer's persona. Like chameleons, they have their own personality, yet change in relation to their environment. Like the balloon blips of the comic strip, they become a dialogue tool, representing something of the wearer, containing some history, serving as indicators of personal mood or attitude. They can also act as talismans, protecting the wearer or imparting magic. Or, they can simply be something special to wear, for no apparent reason. — CAROL WEBB

CAROL WEBB

VALERIAN PIN, 2003

12.7 X 1.9 X 1 CM

COPPER, FINE SILVER, 22-KARAT GOLD;

PHOTOETCHED, SCORED

Photo by Hap Sakwa

CHRISTA LÜHTJE

BROOCH, 1998

3.5 X 1 CM

22-KARAT GOLD

Photo by Eva Jünger

JACQUELINE MYERS

SMALL OVAL 22-KARAT GOLD &
MICROMOSAIC PIN, 2003

2.5 x 2.2 x 0.5 CM

22-KARAT GOLD, ANTIQUE

MICROMOSAIC; HAND-FABRICATED

Photo by Stanley J. Myers

SO YOUNG PARK

UNTITLED, 2003

7 X 7 X 1.3 CM

18-KARAT GOLD, PEARLS

Photo by Jae Man Jo

Omnia Vanitas, meaning "everything is vanity" in Latin, focuses on traditional materials in contemporary jewelry—gold and gems. Selectively taken from the earth, these natural materials are used as commodity. I depict this in the piece by including U.S. currency.

This brooch is meant to deceptively lure the viewer into believing it is just a beautiful piece. Yet upon closer inspection the decorative and seemingly drawn images of leaves are revealed to be pieced foliage from American banknotes. Money infiltrates every aspect of our culture and nature. It also has an attachment to what culture prescribes as valuable and allows me to explore socio-economic issues. — KATHY BUSZKIEWICZ

KATHY BUSZKIEWICZ

OMNIA VANITAS, 2000

5 x 4.1 x 1.3 CM

18-KARAT GOLD, U.S. CURRENCY,
AMETHYST, WOOD;
HAND-FABRICATED, CUT, PIECED

Photo by artist

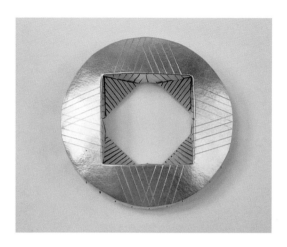

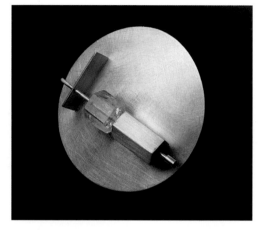

LISA GRALNICK

BROOCH, 2002

1.9 X 7 CM IN DIAMETER

18-KARAT GOLD; FABRICATED

Photo by artist

DAPHNE KRINOS

ROUND BROOCH, 2001

1.1 X 4.5 CM IN DIAMETER

18-KARAT GOLD, AQUAMARINE CRYSTAL BEAD;

ROLLED, HAMMERED, FOLDED

Photo by Joël Degen

LILLY FITZGERALD

PIN, 2002

5.1 CM IN DIAMETER

22-KARAT GOLD, CHALCEDONY;

HAND–FABRICATED

Photo by artist

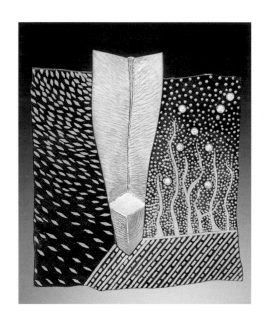

NAMU CHO

MIRAGE 5, 2003

5 X 4.4 CM

DAMASCENE, 22-KARAT GOLD, DIAMONDS

Photo by Hap Sakwa

MELANIE BILENKER

LIKENESS, 2003

3.5 X 2.8 X 1 CM

HAIR, EPOXY RESIN, IVORY PIANO KEY
LAMINATE, STERLING SILVER, EBONY

Photo by Ken Yanoviak

SOOK-HYUN LEE

PLEASURE OF LIGHTNESS III, 2002

EACH, 4 X 4 X 1.5 CM

STERLING SILVER, STAINLESS STEEL, 18-KARAT GOLD, 14-KARAT GOLD; SCORED, SOLDERED

Photo by Myung-Wook Huh (Studio Munch)

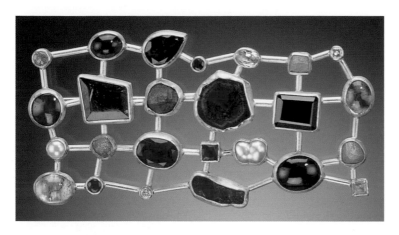

I try to find a contemporary constructivist and painterly approach to the traditional materials and techniques of the goldsmith.

— PETRA CLASS

PETRA CLASS

MOSAIC IN REDS AND YELLOWS, 2003

3.8 X 7.6 X 1.3 CM

18-KARAT GOLD, 22-KARAT GOLD, RUBY,
DIAMOND, YELLOW SAPPHIRE, TOURMALINE,
GARNET, FIRE OPAL, PEARL; FABRICATED

Photo by Hap Sakwa

DAPHNE KRINOS

LOOP BROOCH, 2002

0.6 X 5 CM IN DIAMETER

18-KARAT GOLD, TOURMALINE,
AQUAMARINE CRYSTALS; FORGED

Photo by Joël Degen

BARBARA HEINRICH

AMBER BROOCH, 2003

8 X 5 CM

18-KARAT GOLD, BALTIC AMBER;

HAND–FABRICATED, ROLLER PRINTED

Photo by Tim Callahan

JAN BAUM

LEFT, *SEDUCTION #1*, 1998;

RIGHT, *SEDUCTION #2*, 1998

LEFT, 3.8 X 6.4 X 0.6 CM;

RIGHT, 4.3 X 7.3 X 0.6 CM

18-KARAT GOLD, ENAMEL, SALT,

14-KARAT GOLD, STAINLESS STEEL

Photo by Phil Harris

GIOVANNI CORVAJA

BROOCH, 1998

7 x 7 x 1.2 CM

24-KARAT GOLD, PLATINUM;
GRANULATED

Photos by artist

The animated, matte surface of this brooch reveals, upon closer inspection, thousands of minute, vertically-standing wires, each ending with a tiny spherule of gold, which vibrates when touched.

My inspiration lies in both natural and man-made structures viewed through a microscope. I am also further inspired by technique in itself, and the creative possibilities which emerge when I know how to apply it, research it further, and eventually, push it to extremes.

I feel that many contemporary jewelers erroneously tend to shun technique as inhibiting creativity. This can be so, but it is not always the case. Technical know-how is of fundamental importance in my work; however, it does not dominate my designs. It is merely a means to express an idea freely, with confidence and without compromise if applied with the correct spirit, as a paintbrush might be to a painter. — GIOVANNI CORVAJA

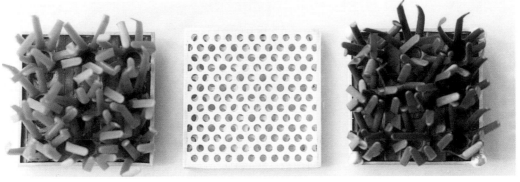

EVA TESARIK

GRASSBROOCHES (GRASS BROOCHES), 1999

EACH, 3.5 X 3.5 X 1 CM

SILVER, PLASTIC

Photos by Barbara Krobath

MARGUERITE CHIANG

IN MY GARDEN, 2003

5.1 X 5.1 CM

STERLING SILVER, OIL PAINT, STAINLESS STEEL;

HAND-FABRICATED, OXIDIZED

Photo by Hap Sakwa

JAN YAGER

WAR ON DRUGS, 2001

0.8 X 7 X 0.8 CM

FOUND PLASTIC CRACK VIAL CAPS, STERLING SILVER;

SORTED, SLICED, FABRICATED

Photo by Jack Ramsdale

IAN BALLY

COLOR CHANGE BROOCH, 2002

6.4 X 6.4 X 1.3 CM

NICKEL SILVER, COLORED FOAM

Photo by artist

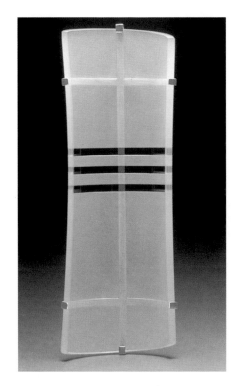

GORDON LAWRIE

STAIRS 2, 1999

6.5 X 4 X 2.5 CM

SILVER; FABRICATED

Photo by artist

DONALD FRIEDLICH

TRANSLUCENCE SERIES BROOCH, 2002

10.2 X 4.1 X 1.9 CM

GLASS, 14-KARAT GOLD, 18-KARAT GOLD;

FABRICATED, CARVED, SANDBLASTED

Photo by James Beards

I n my glass brooches, sandblasting is used to develop varying degrees of transparency in the material. The pieces change color depending on the clothing on which they are worn.

— DONALD FRIEDLICH

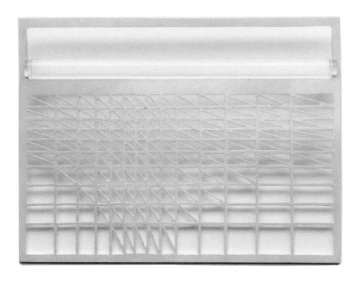

ANTON CEPKA

BROOCH, 2003

5 X 7 X 0.5 CM

SILVER; SOLDERED

Photo by Matúš Cepka

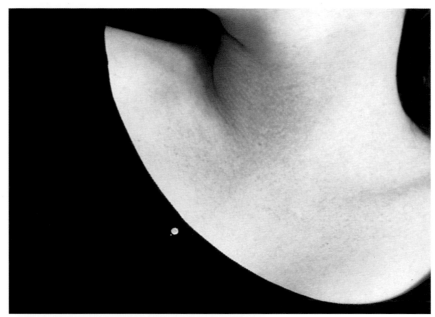

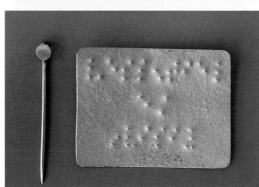

ALYSSA DEE KRAUSS

BRAILLE SERIES: L'ESSENTIEL EST INVISIBLE, 1998

1.9 x 2.5 CM

18-KARAT GOLD

Photo by Kevin Downey

Courtesy of Sienna Gallery,

Lenox, Massachusetts

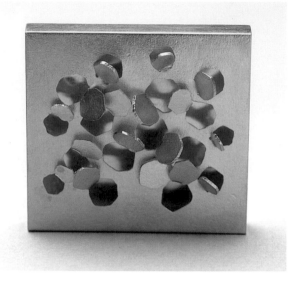

CHRISTEL VAN DER LAAN

REFLEX, 2003

4 X 3.8 X 0.8 CM

18-KARAT GOLD, STERLING SILVER; FABRICATED, PLATED

Photo by Robert Frith

LILLY FITZGERALD

TWINS, 2002

ROUND, 4.4 CM IN DIAMETER

22-KARAT GOLD, DRAGONFLY WINGS, AGATE;

HAND-FABRICATED, CAST

Photo by artist

157

JAN WEHRENS

Brooch, 2001

7.4 x 10.5 x 4.4 CM

SILVER, PATINA

Photo by artist

Babette von Dohnanyi

Pentagonprisma, 2000

2 x 5 x 5 cm

18-karat white gold; soldered

Photo by Federico Cavicchioli

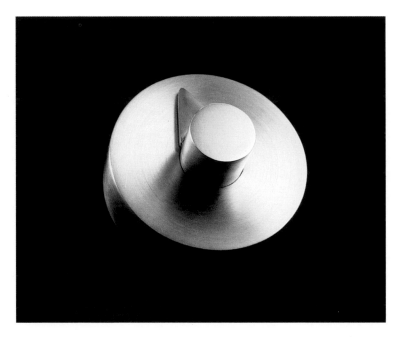

ANNEKE VAN BOMMEL

ARTBOT BACK BROOCH SERIES: DIAL, 2003

4 X 5 X 5 CM

STERLING SILVER; FABRICATED

Photo by artist

OTTO KÜNZLI

FRIEND, 1997

7 CM IN DIAMETER

BRASS; PAINTED

Photo by artist

161

FRANK BÖTTGER

STERLING SILVER AND GOLD BROOCH, 2004

5 x 5 x 0.6 CM

STERLING SILVER, GOLD FOIL; FORMED, SOLDERED

Photo by artist

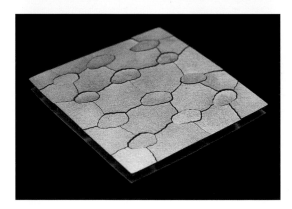

CATHY CHOTARD

UNTITLED, 2003

5 x 5 x 0.4 CM

SILVER

Photo by artist

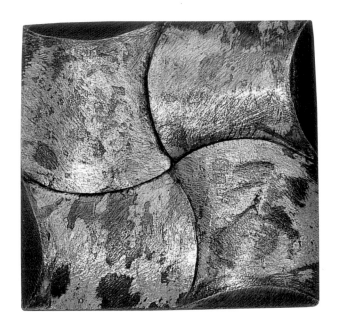

SONDI'S STUDIO

Folded Metaphor, 2003

4 X 4 X 0.7 CM

STERLING SILVER, 24-KARAT GOLD;

HOLLOW CONSTRUCTED

Photo by Richard Walker

MANUEL VILHENA

UNTITLED, 2004

12 X 12 X 4 CM

JUNIPER WOOD, STEEL, PIGMENT;

CARVED, ASSEMBLED, DYED, WAXED

Photo by artist

JENS-RÜDIGER LORENZEN

BROOCH, 2002

5.5 X 5 X 1.2 CM

STEEL, SILVER, PORCELAIN, VARNISH

Photo by Petra Jaschke-Flonheim

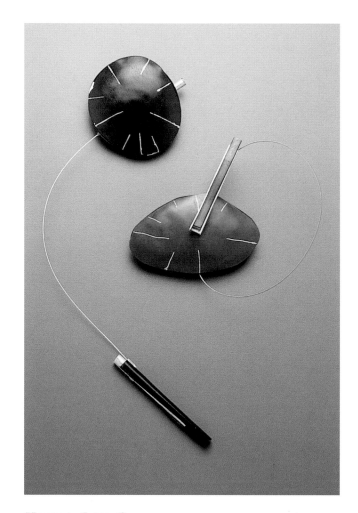

HYUNG-LAN CHOI

ASSOCIATION, 2002

LEFT, 5 x 12.2 x 0.8 CM;

RIGHT, 6.5 x 7 x 1.8 CM

SILVER, COPPER, IVORY, STEEL WIRE

Photo by Myung-Wook Huh (Studio Munch)

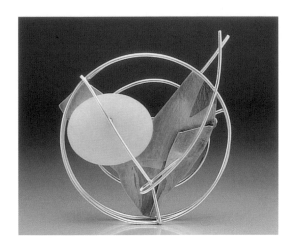

JUNG HEE SHIN

COSMIC TREE, 2000

7.2 x 7.4 x 1.2 CM

Photo by Kwang-Choon Park

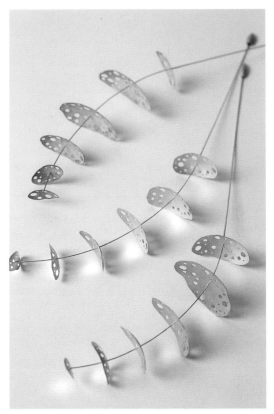

KAYO SAITO

WILD GRASS BROOCH, 2001

EACH, 20 CM

18-KARAT GOLD

Photo by artist

167

JULIA TURNER

UNTITLED, 2001

6.4 X 6.4 X 0.6 CM

EBONY PANEL, GESSO, STERLING SILVER;

SANDED, SCRATCHED

Photo by George Post

JENNIFER JAY FECKER

UNTITLED, WITH MOSS, 2002

1.3 X 6.4 CM IN DIAMETER

14-KARAT YELLOW GOLD, 18-KARAT

YELLOW GOLD, STERLING SILVER,

ACRYLIC, EPOXY, MOSS

Photo by artist

This piece uses drops of epoxy on acrylic to simulate the look of water or condensation, as if the moss grows and thrives just below the surface. — JENNIFER JAY FECKER

MANDY CARROLL

BIG RED, 2002

7.6 X 5.1 CM

FINE SILVER, STERLING SILVER,

ENAMEL, FELT

Photos by Ken Yanoviak

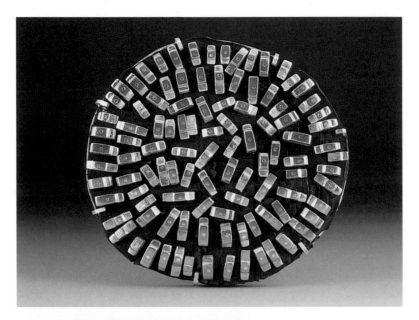

NATALYA PINCHUK

CARS. BROOCH, 2004

7 X 6.4 X 1.9 CM

PEWTER, RUBBER, STERLING SILVER

Photos by artist

SVENJA JOHN

ICE, 2003

7 x 10.8 x 8.6 CM

STAINLESS STEEL, POLYCARBONATE

Photo by Kevin Sprague

Courtesy of Sienna Gallery,

Lenox, Massachusetts

SCOTT CORMIER

BALL SERIES: *LILLY BALL,*
99 CARATS OF STONES ON A BALL,
GOLD BUBBLE BALL, 1998

EACH, 3.8 x 3.8 x 3.8 CM

STERLING SILVER, 18-KARAT GOLD,

SAPPHIRES, ULTRAVIOLET CEMENT;

CONSTRUCTED, SOLDERED

Photo by Rodger Birn

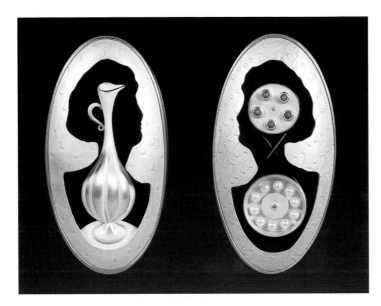

HEATHER WHITE

PROTEAN CAMEO #7,
PROTEAN CAMEO #12, 2000
BOTH, 7.9 X 4.1 X 1.3 CM
22-KARAT GOLD, 18-KARAT GOLD, STERLING
SILVER, VELVET, NICKEL, RUBBER O-RING,
PEARL, RHODOCHROSITE; LOST WAX CAST,
EMBOSSED, DIE FORMED, FABRICATED
Photo by Kyle Dick

My intention with the Protean Cameo *series is to reference historical portraiture jewelry and use the female silhouette as a framing device. With the aid of a computer, I have stretched a clearly feminine, yet generic, silhouette both vertically and horizontally to create many stages of transformation. After hand-piercing the metal, I create recognizable miniature elements to fill each hollow.*

While choosing an object to incorporate, I think about how its meaning will be transformed once inside the feminine silhouette. I also must consider the way an object will physically fit inside the frame to complete the portrait. Many potent objects I would like to frame have various shapes, so it becomes an aesthetic challenge to meet my criteria of form and metaphor. — HEATHER WHITE

JAE-YOUNG KIM

SOUND OF FOREST, 2003

7 X 8 CM

BAMBOO, JADE, SILVER, 18-KARAT GOLD

Photo by Myung-Wook Huh (Studio Munch)

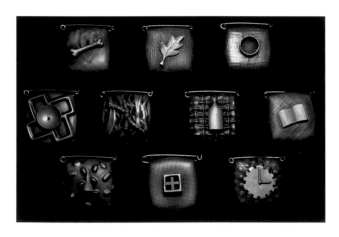

MATTHEW HOLLERN

ICONS BROOCH SERIES, 1997

EACH, 7.6 X 7.6 X 1.3 CM

STERLING SILVER, GOLD,

PEWTER, BRONZE; PRINTED,

FORMED, FABRICATED

Photo by artist

JOHAN VAN ASWEGEN

SHE-SEA, 2000

4 X 4 X 1 CM

ENAMEL, BEACH SAND, MABE PEARLS,

CULTURED PEARLS, 18-KARAT GOLD

Photo by Mark Johnston

Courtesy of Sienna Gallery,

Lenox, Massachusetts

HAROLD O'CONNOR

GRANULATED SEA FAN, 2002

5 X 6.5 X 0.3 CM

18-KARAT GOLD, STERLING SILVER;

EMBOSSED, HAMMERED, GRANULATED

Photo by artist

TODD REED

AMORPHIC DIAMOND CLUSTER #1, 2003

3.8 x 4.4 x 0.6 CM

22-KARAT GOLD, SILVER, STEEL, RAW DIAMONDS,

PRINCESS-CUT DIAMONDS, PATINA;

FORGED, FABRICATED, BRUSH FINISHED

Photo by azadphoto.com

NORIKO SUGAWARA

STARRY NIGHT, 2003

5 X 5 X 0.8 CM

SHAKUDO, 24-KARAT GOLD, 18-KARAT GOLD, DIAMOND, SOUTH SEA PEARL; INLAID

Photos by artist

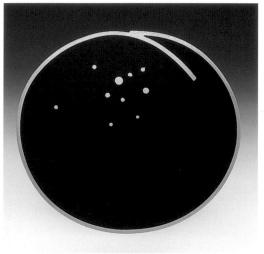

STEPHANE THRELKELD

MORNING GLORY, 2004

5 X 10 X 10 CM

STAINLESS STEEL MESH, PLATINUM, DIAMOND;

FOLDED, CONSTRUCTED

Photo by Monte Trístan

JOHN IVERSEN

ENAMEL PIN, 2003

8.9 X 7.6 X 0.2 CM

18-KARAT GOLD, ENAMEL

Photo by Kenji-Ishii

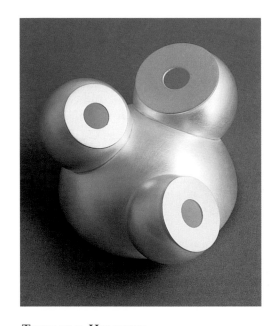

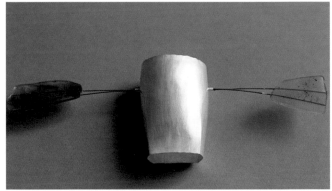

THERESE HILBERT

HOLLOW BUT NOT EMPTY, 1999

4.4 X 5.5 CM IN DIAMETER

SILVER

Photo by Otto Künzli

ULRIKE KLEINE-BEHNKE

FLYER, 2003

8 X 15 X 4.5 CM

SILVER, STEEL, PLASTIC; FORGED

Photo by artist

MARIA PHILLIPS

REMINDER #1, 2003

11.4 X 2.5 X 5 CM

COPPER, ENAMEL, STEEL, SILVER,
18-KARAT GOLD, SAFETY PIN;
ELECTROFORMED,
FABRICATED, PLATED

Photo by Doug Yaple

The process of electroforming allows me to capture, and give permanence to, an object that otherwise would vanish. The preserved, enhanced result denotes a moment, a memory, something of significance.

— MARIA PHILLIPS

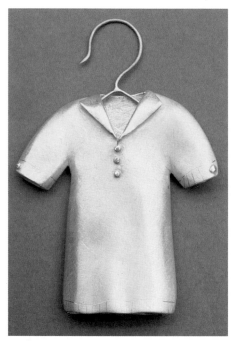

WINFRIED KRUEGER

5 BROOCHES, 2000

LARGEST, 5 X 10 CM

SILVER, ENAMEL

Photo by artist

JOHANNA BECKER-BLACK

HANGING SHIRT BROOCH, 2003

6.4 X 3.2 X 1.3 CM

STERLING SILVER, 18-KARAT GOLD;

FABRICATED

Photo by James Hart

Katja Prins

Cocoon Brooches, 1999

Average, 6 x 2.5 x 2.5 cm

Silver, silk cocoons, polyurethane rubber

Photo by Gerhard Jaeger

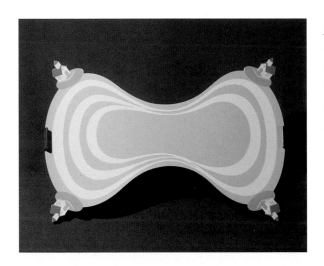

NORMAN WEBER

HAUS & GARTEN #5
(HOUSE & GARDEN #5), 2002
6.4 X 12.4 X 2.1 CM
SILVER, STEEL, C-PRINT
Photo by artist

PARK SUNG-SOOK

HOUSE WITH SKY BALLOON, 2003
LARGEST, 6.5 X 9.5 CM
SILVER, COPPER, FILM
Photo by Myung-Wook Huh (Studio Munch)

ANGELA GLEASON

DEVELOPMENT (9 BROOCHES), 1998
GROUPING, 7 x 45.7 x 1.3 CM
SILVER, COPPER, GOLD LEAF, PLASTIC,
WOOD, GUT, FOUND OBJECTS, GLASS,
STEEL, ALUMINUM, LEAD
Photos by Jeff Van Kleeck

REINA MIA BRILL

ENLIL, 2004

13.3 X 7.6 X 2.5 CM

EPOXY RESIN, WIRE, NICKEL;

MACHINE-KNITTED

Photo by artist

ROB JACKSON

THE GREEN DOOR, 1990

5.1 X 3 X 0.6 CM

SILVER, COPPER, GOLD, BRASS, SAPPHIRE,

MICA; HOLLOW CONSTRUCTED, CHASED,

ENGRAVED, RIVETED, SPRING HINGED

Photo by artist

KEITH A. LEWIS

RAPTURE, 1997

9 X 4.5 X 3 CM

STERLING SILVER, ACRYLIC, PAINT

Photos by artist

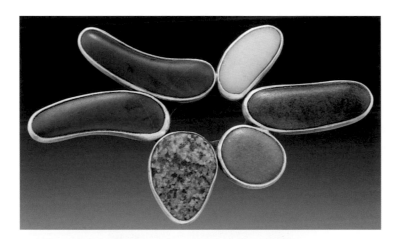

TERRI LOGAN

MEGA, 2003

5 x 8.9 x 1.3 CM

RIVER ROCK, FINE SILVER,
STERLING SILVER, PATINA;
BEZELED, BRUSH FINISHED

Photo by Jerry Anthony

ANN JENKINS

THREE ELEMENTS BROOCH, 2002

5 x 8.9 x 0.6 CM

24-KARAT GOLD LEAF, FINE SILVER,
STERLING SILVER, COPPER, GLASS, ACRYLIC,
DRIED SEED POD, CORAL, GUINEA FOWL FEATHERS;
CARVED, CHASED, FABRICATED, RIVETED

Photo by Robert Diamante

JUDITH HOYT

ORANGE & WHITE STRIPS, 2004

11.4 x 4.7 x 0.3 CM

FOUND METAL, COPPER, STAINLESS STEEL;

RIVETED, HAND-FABRICATED

Photo by John Lenz

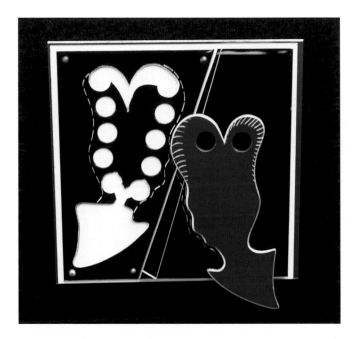

DAVID LAPLANTZ

SPLIT DICHOTOMY BROOCH, 1995

7 X 6.4 X 0.6 CM

ALUMINUM, IRON; PAINTED,

FABRICATED, RIVETED, ENGRAVED

Photo by artist

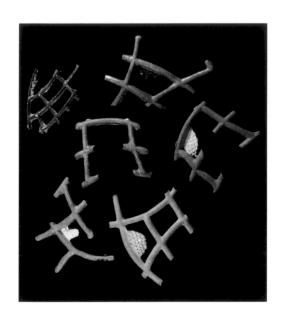

WINFRIED KRUEGER

6 BROOCHES, 2000

EACH, 6 X 7 CM

SILVER, ENAMEL

Photo by artist

MIKE HOLMES

BROOCH, 2003

8.9 X 6.4 X 5.1 CM

WALNUT, GESSO, GOLD LEAF, PIGMENTS,

BRASS, STERLING SILVER; CARVED

Photo by Jeffrey Goldsmith

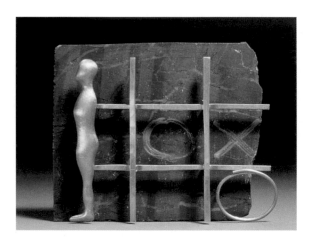

JUNG-HOO KIM

THE OX GAME, 1997

6.7 X 7.8 X 1.9 CM

STERLING SILVER, NATIVE STONE,

24-KARAT GOLD; KUM BOO

Photo by In-Shik Kim

FRANK BÖTTGER

CERAMIC AND STERLING SILVER BROOCH, 1989

9 X 9 X 0.8 CM

CERAMIC, STERLING SILVER

Photo by artist

MONICA CECCHI

LOVE PARK, 2003

8 X 6 X 1.6 CM

18-KARAT WHITE GOLD, 18-KARAT GOLD,

TIN CAN, WOOD; CONSTRUCTED

Photo by Federico Cavicchioli

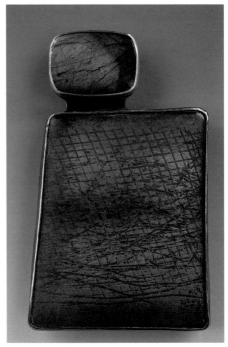

TAWEESAK MOLSAWAT

TIME SERIES: ARTICLE NO. 1: THE CONDITION OF BEING A HUMAN, 2002

7.6 X 7.6 X 1.3 CM

STERLING SILVER, ENAMEL, COPPER, LAZERTRAN®, SALT, RED PEPPER, FOUND OBJECTS

Photo by artist

LENI FUHRMAN

LAVA SERIES #2, 2000

7.2 X 2.5 X 1 CM

ENAMEL, COPPER, FINE SILVER, STERLING SILVER, 22-KARAT GOLD, PEARL; ROLLER PRINTED, FABRICATED

Photo by Erik S. Lieber

GISBERT STACH

AMBER FROM THE FUTURE—INCLUSION V, 1998

2 X 10 X 1.9 CM

LUCITE, INK CARTRIDGE, STEEL

Photo by artist

KIM JOON-HEE

THE WIND, 2003

10 x 11 x 5 CM

SILVER, ACRYLIC; SOLDERED

Photo by Myung-Wook Huh (Studio Munch)

JIN-HEE JUNG

WHISPERING BROOCH II, 2003

EACH, 10 X 3 X 4.5 CM

SILVER, GOLD

Photo by Myung-Wook Huh (Studio Munch)

JOHANNA BECKER-BLACK

FLOWER POT BROOCH, 2003

5.1 X 1.9 X 1.3 CM

STERLING SILVER, 14-KARAT GOLD,

18-KARAT GOLD, EPOXY RESIN,

DIRT; FABRICATED

Photo by James Hart

JACQUELINE RYAN

PIN, 2002

12 x 3.8 x 0.7 CM

18-KARAT GOLD; PIERCED, SOLDERED

Photo by Giovanni Corvaja

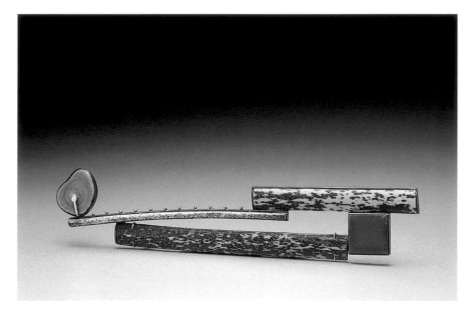

Jae-Young Kim

The Other Way, 2003

3.5 x 15 cm

Bamboo, coral, jade, silver, 18-karat gold

Photo by Myung-Wook Huh (Studio Munch)

The design of this brooch came from the ground plan of a house, built in 1830, where my family came from.

— ANNA EICHLINGER

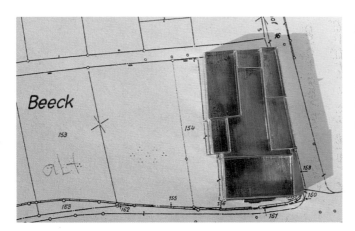

ANNA EICHLINGER

BEECK, 2000

7 x 4 x 0.4 CM

22-KARAT GOLD;
CONSTRUCTED

Photo by artist

MONICA CECCHI

THE KEY, 2001

4 x 2.5 x 1 CM

18-KARAT GOLD, FOUND OBJECT;
CONSTRUCTED

Photo by Federico Cavicchioli

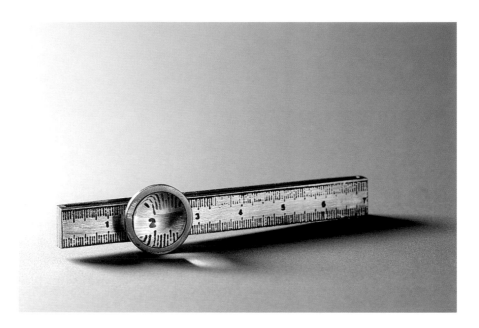

MYOUNG SUN LEE

PSYCHOLOGICAL DISTANCE 3, 2003

0.8 X 7 X 0.8 CM

SILVER

Photo by Myung-Wook Huh (Studio Munch)

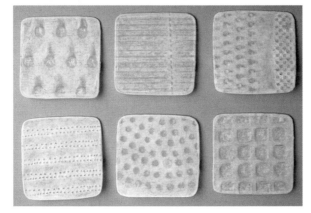

FRANCINE HAYWOOD

DOMESTICITY, 2000

EACH, 4.5 X 4.5 CM

TOILET PAPER, SILVER; FABRICATED, TEXTURED

Photos by artist

*T*his series of six paper brooches illustrates conflicting feelings: as simple squares of flimsy white paper, they point out the futility of monotonous, repetitive, domestic acts, while celebrating their unique, ephemeral, unrecognized beauty. The medium I used, toilet paper, is a common, valueless, disposable material. It has been textured to reproduce the surface of familiar cooking utensils, like graters, potato mashers, sushi mats, etc. I wet-cast the paper directly onto those objects, using water and PVA glue. The texture is delicate and subtle, its perception changing with the play of light and movements of the wearer.

—— FRANCINE HAYWOOD

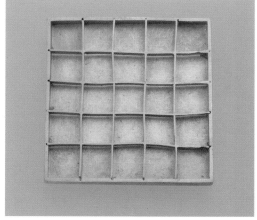

BILLIE JEAN THEIDE

BLACK AND WHITE RUIN, 2003

8.3 CM IN DIAMETER

STERLING SILVER; CAST, FABRICATED, OXIDIZED

Photo by artist

EMMA WOOD

ELEVATOR VENT, 2003

3.8 X 3.8 X 0.3 CM

18-KARAT GOLD; CONSTRUCTED

Photo by artist

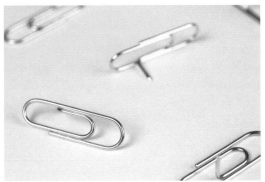

JIRO KAMATA

CLIP PIN, 2002

1 X 2 X 0.5 CM

18-KARAT GOLD

Photos by artist

BEN NEUBAUER

PIN, 2003

2.5 X 7.6 X 1.3 CM

STERLING SILVER,
18-KARAT YELLOW GOLD

Photo by Courtney Frisse

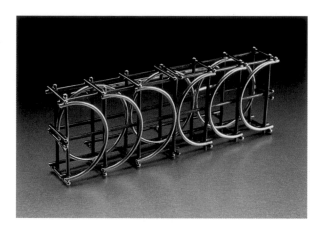

DONNA D'AQUINO

WIRE BROOCH #15, 2001

3.8 X 12.7 X 2.5 CM

18-KARAT GOLD, STEEL;
HAND-FABRICATED

Photo by Ralph Gabriner

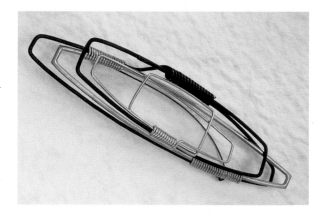

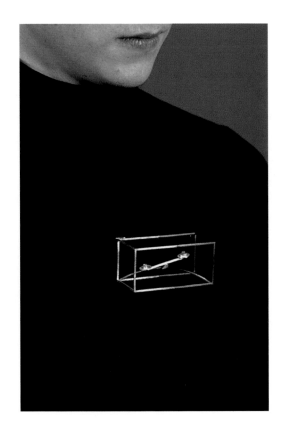

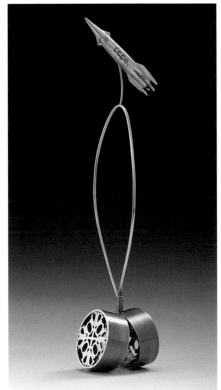

LIAUNG-CHUNG YEN

AVERAGE JOE, 2004

3.5 X 7 X 3.5 CM

14-KARAT GOLD, SILVER,

DIAMOND, ROUGH DIAMOND

Photo by Dan Neuberger

SUSAN R. EWING

BOHEMIAN TRAJECTORY BROOCH, 2000

12.7 X 2.5 X 2.2 CM

STERLING SILVER, 18-KARAT GOLD,

FOUND PLASTIC TOY; FABRICATED

Photo by Jeffrey Sabo

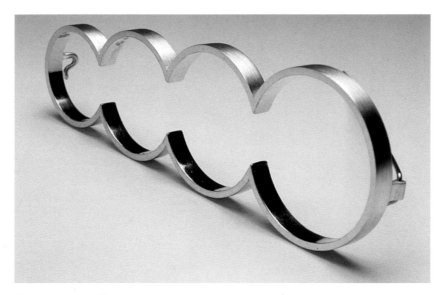

ELIZABETH BONE

GROWTH RING BROOCH, 2000

8 CM LONG

SILVER, 18-KARAT GOLD, STEEL; FABRICATED, PLATED

Photo by Joël Degen

KIKKAN HULTHÉN

UNTITLED, 2001

14.5 X 1.9 CM IN DIAMETER

ALUMINUM, PLASTIC, COTTON T-SHIRT; HANDPRINTED

Photo by Annika Åkerfelt

THOMAS DIERKS

VEHICLE, 2000

1.5 X 3.5 X 7 CM

STERLING SILVER, BLUE TOPAZ, LEAD; CAST

Photo by artist

KEITH A. LEWIS

PERSEPHONE'S SAD FEAST, 1999

7 X 4 X 3 CM

STERLING SILVER, COPPER, NICKEL SILVER,

18-KARAT GOLD, 24-KARAT GOLD; PLATED

Photo by Doug Yaple

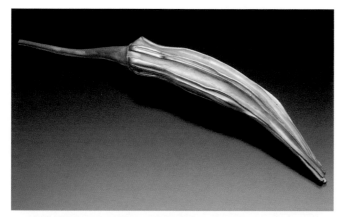

JENNIFER HALL

OKRA, 1998

12.7 x 1.6 x 1.3 cm

STERLING SILVER; FABRICATED

Photo by Doug Yaple

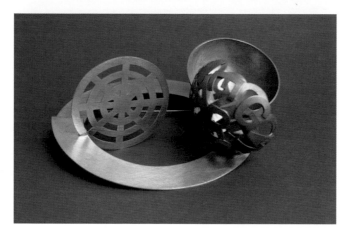

JAN WEHRENS

BROOCH, 2003

6 x 14.5 x 13 cm

STEEL, SILVER, PATINA

Photo by artist

Agnes Kainz

Untitled, 2003

6.5 x 13 x 5 cm

Aluminum, steel; assembled

Photo by Manuel Vilhena

KIM JOON-HEE

A WHEEL, 2003

12 X 9 X 4 CM

SILVER, ACRYLIC; SOLDERED

Photo by Myung-Wook Huh (Studio Munch)

SHIN HEA-RIM

THE VISUAL STORY, 2003

9.5 x 11 x 1.3 CM

STERLING SILVER, PATINA; FABRICATED, PAINTED

Photo by Myung-Wook Huh (Studio Munch)

The Animal Relationships: 21st Century *brooch is a commentary on the social evolution of dogs and cats. Animals sharing our homes can't recall how their ancestors roamed using their survival skills. Our animals are modern. They take out a health insurance policy in the form of a human. The image depicts healthy, stress-free pets.*

The design of the outer brooch summarizes its concept; the inner part pivots—one side showing the image as the other explains the evolution. The wearer may display either the image or the text as the primary ornament.

— NANCY MOYER

NANCY MOYER

ANIMAL RELATIONSHIPS: 21ST CENTURY, 2004

0.6 X 5.7 CM IN DIAMETER

COPPER, SILVER, DECALS, ACRYLIC SHEET, GLASS;

SOLDERED, RIVETED, MARRIED METALS

Photo by artist

LISA AND SCOTT CYLINDER

PENCILATED WOODPECKER BROOCH, 2004

12.7 X 7.6 X 0.6 CM

STERLING SILVER, BRASS, COMPASS, ANTIQUE

WOODEN DOMINOES, PENCILS, EPOXY RESIN;

FORMED, FABRICATED

Photo by Jeffrey K. Brady

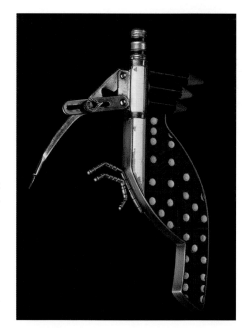

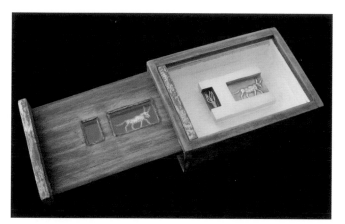

JUDY McCAIG

CROSSING, 2002

BOX: 7 X 10.5 X 3.5 CM; BROOCH: 3 X 4.5 X 0.5 CM

WOOD, GOLD LEAF, THERMOPLASTIC, SILVER, 18-KARAT GOLD,

22-KARAT GOLD; STAINED, CARVED, PRESS FORMED

Photos by artist

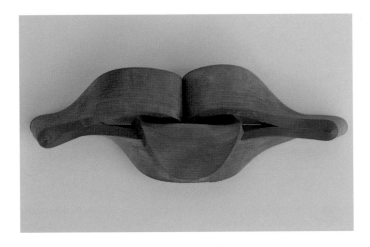

DAVID BIELANDER

LIP, 2000

4 X 8 X 4 CM

RUBBER SEAL, STEEL

Photo by artist

PHILIP SAJET

MOTHERBROOCH, 1995

6 X 6 X 0.5 CM

SILVER, GOLD, ENAMEL, RUBY

Photo by artist

These brooches represent a recent departure for me. They are neither narrative nor conceptual jewelry. Instead, I want to operate within the traditional parameters and expectations of Western jewelry to make objects that are decorative and comfortably wearable. Beyond that, I want these articles to become the center of attention when they are worn, and thus to make their wearers feel exceptional.

The forms are derived from drawings, and ultimately look back to cartoons. Some of the images are of flowers and leaves, which are thought to have been the earliest jewelry, and which continue to play an important role in the beautification of the human body. Other forms are taken from biology, body parts, letters, the history of the Decorative Arts, or sheer invention. — BRUCE METCALF

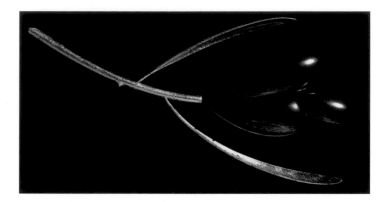

BRUCE METCALF

KISSBLOOM 2, 2003

14 x 9.5 CM

MAPLE, BRASS, GOLD; CARVED, PAINTED, FORGED, CHASED, PLATED

Photo by artist

GREGORÉ MOŔIN

CANADA GOOSE—FLYING SOUTH, 2001

3.5 x 7.5 x 0.9 CM

EMERALD, DIAMOND, CARNELIAN, GOLD, PLATINUM;

HAND-FABRICATED

Photo by Nino Rakichevich

NATHANIEL DELARGE

11-06-03, 2003

12.7 x 3.8 x 5 CM

SILVER, PLASTIC DEER, BRASS BELL

Photos by Don Brazil

THOMAS HILL

BUTTERFLY FISH, FROM THE SERIES
X-RAY FISH, 2003
10.2 X 11.4 X 0.6 CM
COW BONE, BRASS WIRE;
SCRIMSHAWED, FABRICATED
Photo by Jeffrey Goldsmith

SILVIA WALZ

BERTA, 2003

12 x 2.5 x 1.2 cm

SILVER, PLASTIC, PHOTOGRAPH, PORCELAIN

Photo by Ramon Puig Cuyàs

B*erta,*

of light feet, but heavy legs

This has the advantage, that she
doesn't fall that easy

The churning in her belly is chronic

She draws on plentiful resources
without looking.

— SILVIA WALZ

ULO FLORACK

BROOCH

7 X 5 X 1 CM

ENAMEL, GOLD, METAL ALLOY; PLATED

Photo by artist

FLORIAN BUDDEBERG

SILVER PAINTED, 2003

9 X 4 X 2 CM

SILVER; PAINTED

Photo by artist

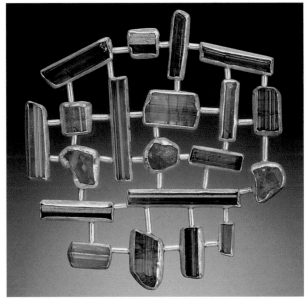

LOLA BROOKS

Brooch, 2003

4 x 3 x 2.2 CM

STAINLESS STEEL, VINTAGE ROSE-CUT
GARNETS, 18-KARAT GOLD;
HOLLOW CONSTRUCTED, SOLDERED

Photo by Dean Powell

PETRA CLASS

Mosaic in Green—Homage à Mondrian, 2002

6.4 x 6.4 x 1.3 CM

18-KARAT GOLD, 22-KARAT GOLD, TOURMALINE,
DIAMOND, IMPERIAL TOPAZ; FABRICATED

Photo by Hap Sakwa

KIM RAWDIN

BROOCH, 2000

8.9 x 10.2 x 2.5 CM

18-KARAT GOLD, 22-KARAT GOLD, LAPIS LAZULI, CORAL, RHODINITE,

CHRYSOPRASE, SUGALITE, RUTILATED QUARTZ, JADE, BLACK ONYX;

HOLLOW CONSTRUCTED, HAND-FABRICATED

Photo by artist

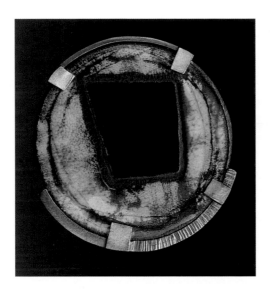

JAN SMITH

BLUE RECTANGLE WITHIN CIRCLE, 2002

4.1 X 0.6 CM

ENAMEL, COPPER, STERLING SILVER,

22-KARAT GOLD BIMETAL;

CHAMPLEVÉ, SGRAFFITO

Photo by Doug Yaple

I am interested in the surface nuances of textiles, botanical forms, and eroded surfaces. I use the enamel to build layers of images, colors, and marks, generally working in a series, using recurring elements as one would familiar words to address my response to these objects. The recurring elements are meant to evoke memories, layers of varied emotions, and past experiences. The layers of transparent colors and the luminescence of them never fail to seduce me. Enamel and etching allow me to incorporate a drawing sensibility into my work. My work is process-oriented in that I begin with a feeling that I want the piece to evoke rather than with a formal, completed design. — JAN SMITH

BARBARA MINOR

RED STONES CIRCLE WITH MATTE ONYX AND

CARNELIAN, 2002

7.6 X 7.6 X 0.6 CM

OPAQUE ENAMEL, COPPER, MATTE ONYX,

MATTE CARNELIAN, SILVER

Photo by Ralph Gabriner

DONNA D'AQUINO

SCATTER PINS, 2003

1.3 TO 6.4 CM

STEEL, PLASTIC; HAND-FABRICATED, DIPPED

Photo by Ralph Gabriner

My work is based on line and the act of drawing. It is inspired by interior and exterior skeletal structures in architecture. — DONNA D'AQUINO

SCOTT CORMIER

OVERLAPPING CIRCLE BROOCH SERIES, 1997

EACH, 6.4 X 6.4 X 1.3 CM

18-KARAT GOLD, STERLING SILVER, SAPPHIRES,

RUBIES, PEARLS, ULTRAVIOLET CEMENT; SOLDERED

Photo by Rodger Birn

VANESSA SAMUELS

Somethin' Bloomin' #1 & #2, 2003

LARGEST, 0.2 X 9 CM IN DIAMETER

STERLING SILVER, STAINLESS STEEL; OXIDIZED

Photo by artist

CHARRA JAROSZ

BROOCHES IN THE SAUCHIEHALL SERIES, 2003

EACH, 7 X 2.5 X 1.9 CM

STERLING SILVER, 18-KARAT GOLD, 22-KARAT GOLD; FABRICATED

Photo by Doug Yaple

Perplexed by the body and its organization, I am curious about architectures that house the body and the architectonic body; my formal decisions take place within this intersection.

This group of work was conceived during a trip to my grandfather's native Scotland, where I was reacquainted with the inspiring architecture of Glasgow's favorite son, Charles Rennie Mackintosh.

— CHARRA JAROSZ

JENNIFER CRUPI

EXPANDABLE BROOCH, 1997

2.5 x 12.7 CM IN DIAMETER

STERLING SILVER; HOLLOW CONSTRUCTED, RIVETED

Photos by Christian Luis

E xpandable Brooch *is part of a series of jewelry in which I investigated mechanical movement, expandable structures in particular. The exploration stemmed from my interest in making jewelry that is interactive—that doesn't merely sit on the body in one fixed way but can constantly be manipulated and transformed (in size, shape, or function) by the wearer. At the same time, the pieces are meant to incite a curiosity that would encourage interaction from viewers as well.* — JENNIFER CRUPI

T. J. LECHTENBERG

CIRCLE BROOCH #1, 2002

7.6 X 7.6 X 2.5 CM

NICKEL, BRASS, ACRYLIC, STERLING SILVER;

FABRICATED, PLATED

Photos by Kee-ho Yuen

MANUELA SOUSA

UNTITLED, 2004

EACH, 3.5 X 2.5 X 2 CM

SILVER, TITANIUM, ALUMINUM; COLORED, ANODIZED

Photos by artist

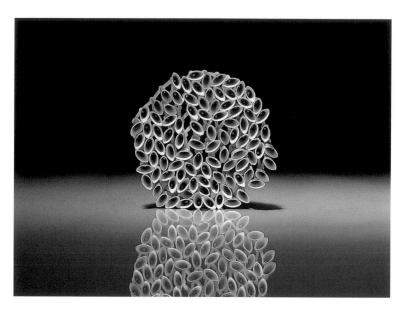

JACQUELINE RYAN

BROOCH, 1999

6 CM IN DIAMETER

18-KARAT GOLD, ENAMEL

Photo by Giovanni Corvaja

*I*n my work, I abstract nature and seek to communicate brief impressions of what I have observed and encountered. Working from sketches made from life, I collect visual information from the abundance of forms, surfaces, textures, structures, and colors of which nature is infinitely rich. I translate these into paper models before moving on to the final piece.

Much of my work is made up of loosely fixed moveable elements that shake and jangle as the body moves. The interaction of the wearer with the work completes its function and brings it to life.

— JACQUELINE RYAN

CATHY CHOTARD

UNTITLED, 2003

5.5 X 7.6 X 1 CM

SILVER

Photo by artist

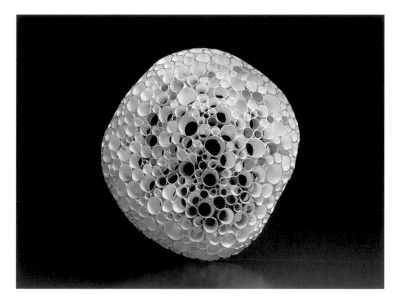

ANYA PINCHUK

BROOCH, 2003

7.6 x 7.6 x 2.5 CM

SILVER; SOLDERED

Photo by artist

EMILY WATSON

THE GRAPHIC BODY ATTACHABLE NO. 2, 2003

12 x 5.1 x 4.4 CM

COPPER, ENAMEL, STEEL, MAGNETS;

ELECTROFORMED, CONSTRUCTED

Photo by artist

ANYA KIVARKIS

BROOCH, 2003

7 X 5.5 X 3.5 CM

COPPER, ENAMEL, STERLING SILVER;

DIE FORMED, FABRICATED

Photo by artist

ANYA KIVARKIS

BROOCH, 2003

6 X 4.5 X 3.5 CM

COPPER, ENAMEL, STERLING SILVER;

FORMED

Photo by artist

SVENJA JOHN

BREATH BROOCH, 2001

4 X 9 CM IN DIAMETER

POLYCARBONATE; SURFACE TREATED,

CONSTRUCTED, COLORED

Photo by Silke Mayer

DANIEL KRUGER

UNTITLED, 2003

8 X 9 X 4 CM

STERLING SILVER, TURQUOISE CHIPS, CORAL;

FORGED, HINGED, KNOTTED

Photo by Nikolaus Brade

HYE-YOUNG SUH

*BGE*22*, 2003

7.6 X 7.6 X 2.5 CM

ENAMEL, COPPER, STERLING SILVER;

ELECTROFORMED

Photo by artist

BRIDGET CATCHPOLE

HAIRY DONUT, 2002

3.5 X 7.6 X 3.5 CM

STERLING SILVER, SYNTHETIC BRISTLES; REPOUSSÉ

Photo by Anthony McLean

BEPPE KESSLER

UPS AND DOWNS, 2002

EACH, 3.5 X 3.5 X 1.5 CM

BALSA WOOD, COTTON, PALLADIUM, GLASS, CRYSTAL BEADS;
BURNED, EMBROIDERED

Photo by Taco Anema

The material is the vehicle of my thoughts.

Working is a way of life to create my own language and explore the limits of what can be called jewelry. Meaning plays an important part, but, on the other hand, I do not want the pieces to be too easy to read.

I do not work with pure gold and silver but prefer to use materials that are less burdened with the traditions of jewelry. I am looking for a kind of mystery in the material, and I try to seduce people to come closer and touch it—at first only with their eyes, then by wearing my jewelry closer to their hearts, hands, and skin.

— BEPPE KESSLER

239

*I*n my most recent work I have used flowers as symbols of appreciation and as offerings and tributes. The floral elements are precisely arranged to become the contents of what I call shrines. This series of little shrines was inspired by the need for reminders that natural beauty exists, to be contemplated and admired.　— GISELLE KOLB

GISELLE KOLB

SET OF FIVE BROOCHES, 2001

EACH, 2.5 X 2.5 X 1.9 CM

STERLING SILVER, FINE SILVER, ENAMEL, 18-KARAT GOLD, WOOD, SAND; HAND-FABRICATED

Photo by Peter Groesbeck

MARY PRESTON

CAMEO CHIMERA, 2002

4.4 X 2.5 X 0.6 CM

18-KARAT GOLD, SILVER, CUT STEEL, PEARLS;
FABRICATED, REPOUSSÉ

Photo by Ralph Gabriner

CORNELIA GOLDSMITH

TREEBROOCH—OLD GROWTH, 2002

4.4 X 4.8 CM

18-KARAT GOLD, 18-KARAT WHITE GOLD,
ORANGE SAPPHIRES, EMERALDS, DIAMONDS;
FABRICATED, CHASED

Photo by Hap Sakwa

PIERRE CAVALAN

DIEU EST MON DROIT, 1994

18.5 X 12 X 3.5 CM

FOUND OBJECTS; ASSEMBLED

Photo by Julian Wolkenstein

KATHLEEN BROWNE

THE GOLD GLOVE, 2002

8.9 X 5 X 0.6 CM

FINE SILVER, STERLING SILVER,

ENAMEL DECAL; FABRICATED

Photo by artist

This series of brooches is intended to be worn on the back and allude to the mechanism found on wind-up tin toys and talking dolls of the past and present. They represent my concern for recognizing processes in life and emphasize our humanity—or lack of—in contemporary society.

— ANNEKE VAN BOMMEL

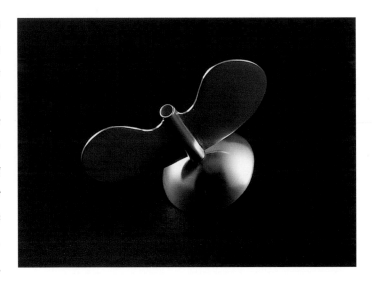

ANNEKE VAN BOMMEL

ARTBOT BACK BROOCH SERIES: TURN, 2003

5 X 7 X 4 CM

STERLING SILVER; CONSTRUCTED, FABRICATED

Photo by artist

This brooch reminds us of the preciousness of our world and the fluidity of its constellation. The globe is a large gem, and the continents are gold and free floating.

— SONDRA SHERMAN

SONDRA SHERMAN

CONTINENTAL DRIFT, 1998

3 x 5.7 x 0.5 CM

STERLING SILVER, 22-KARAT GOLD, ACETATE,

WATER, GLASS; CONSTRUCTED

Photo by artist

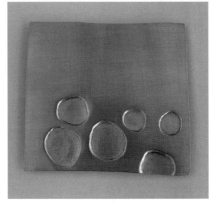

KAROL WEISSLECHNER

BROOCH, 2003

7.5 X 6.5 X 1 CM

SILVER, SYNTHETIC LAPIS LAZULI, GOLD, PATINA

Photo by Pavol Janek

ULRIKE KLEINE-BEHNKE

LANDSCAPE, 2001

7 X 7.5 X 0.2 CM

SILVER; HAMMERED

Photo by artist

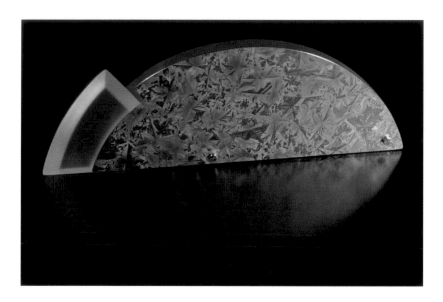

KAREN MCCREARY

Pulse Vector, 2000

5.1 x 14 x 1.3 cm

ACRYLIC, GALVANIZED STEEL, STERLING SILVER, DIODES;

CARVED, FABRICATED

Photo by artist

MARJORIE SCHICK

FOR WANT OF A NAIL, 2001

CANVAS BROOCHES: 25.4 X 5.7 X 3.8;

STICK PINS: 16.5 X 2.5 CM

CANVAS, WOOD, STAINLESS STEEL WIRE;

STITCHED, STUFFED, PAINTED

Photos by Gary Pollmiller

NANNA MELLAND

FRAGMENT OF LIFE II, 2003

6 X 3.5 X 3.5 CM

PLASTIC, STERLING SILVER, GLASS;

CAST, HAND-BLOWN

Photos by artist

JACQUELINE RYAN

BROOCH, 2000

6 CM IN DIAMETER

18-KARAT GOLD; FABRICATED

Photo by Giovanni Corvaja

PAVEL HERYNEK

RENAISSANCE III, 2002

4 X 6 X 2.2 CM

BRASS, STAINLESS STEEL; GILDED

Photo by Markéta Ondrusková

CLAUDE SCHMITZ

BOX, 2002

0.8 X 6.3 CM IN DIAMETER

STERLING SILVER, PATINA

Photo by Christian Mosar

CLAUDE SCHMITZ

RING, 2002

1.3 X 6.4 CM IN DIAMETER

STERLING SILVER, PATINA

Photo by Christian Mosar

Silke Trekel

Brooches Ost und West

(Brooches East and West), 1996

Left, 0.8 x 7 cm in diameter

Nickel silver, gold leaf; hammered

Photo by Helga Schulze-Brinkop

NANCY MOYER

THE HUNTER-GATHERER: 21ST CENTURY, 2004

0.6 X 5.7 CM IN DIAMETER

COPPER, SILVER, DECAL, COMPUTER PRINT,

ACRYLIC SHEET, GLASS; SOLDERED, RIVETED,

MARRIED METALS

Photo by artist

The Social Evolution Brooches thoughtfully address selected aspects of evolution. This particular brooch is a commentary on evolutionary change in the concept of hunting and gathering. The modern hunter is a shopper whose hunting skills are exercised within the walls of stores. Gathering is mostly decision-making in the land of plenty. The image depicts a modern shopper gathering food from the "hunt."

— NANCY MOYER

JIRO KAMATA

TESA BROOCH, 2003

3 x 7 x 1.5 CM

TAPE, SILVER

Photos by artist

WIM VAN DOORSCHODT

WITH LOVE, 2003

6.5 x 13 x 1 CM

ACRYLIC; LAMINATED

Photo by Tom Noz

MAH RANA

BALLOON FLOWER, 2001

EACH, 12 X 2.5 X 2.5 CM

RUBBER, STEEL, POLYESTER CORD

Photo by Colin Campbell

CORNELIA GOLDSMITH

BUTTERFLY BROOCH, 2002

3.8 x 5.7 CM

22-KARAT GOLD, 18-KARAT GOLD, PLATINUM,
RED AND BLUE SAPPHIRES, DIAMONDS;
FABRICATED, DIE FORMED, CHASED, GRANULATED

Photo by Ralph Gabriner

JACLYN DAVIDSON

WINTER SERIES POPPY, 2004

12.7 x 3.8 x 3.2 CM

18-KARAT GOLD, PAVÉ DIAMONDS;
HAND-FORMED, CAST, CHASED,
ENGRAVED, FINISHED

Photo by Ralph Gabriner

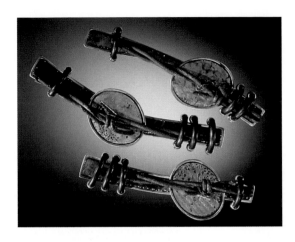

JAN ARTHUR HARRELL

VERTEBRAE SERIES BROOCHES, 2001

EACH, 8.9 X 3.8 X 1.3 CM

STERLING SILVER, COPPER, ENAMEL,

24-KARAT GOLD, BARBED WIRE,

RUBBER CORD

Photo by Jack B. Zilker

This work addresses the aging of our bodies, represented by dark patinas, rust, and ordinary found objects. The use of bright colors and textured gold foils, however, also speaks of the ageless human spirit.

— JAN ARTHUR HARRELL

STEPHEN ROBISON

PENGA, 2002–2003

5.1 X .6 CM

ENAMEL, STERLING SILVER; ELECTROFORMED,

FABRICATED, CHAMPLEVÉ

Photo by artist

The house brooches are designed as part of my ideal retirement village for textile artists.

— JANICE ELIZABETH APPLETON

JANICE ELIZABETH APPLETON

SHELLEY'S HOUSE, 2003

5.5 x 5 x 0.5 CM

FABRIC, BEADS; MACHINE EMBROIDERED

Photo by artist

BERNHARD SCHOBINGER

PEARL OUT OF THE TUBE, 2002

6.9 X 1.7 X 0.9 CM

TAHITIAN PEARL, CHROMIUM,

ALUMINUM TUBE, PAINT; PRINTED

Photo by P. Voellmy

Courtesy of Gallery Von Bartha,

Basel, Switzerland

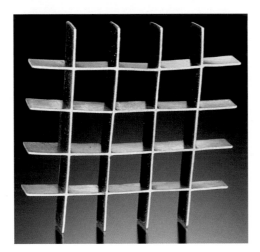

MARGUERITE CHIANG

THE ROOMS IN MY HOUSE, 2003

5.1 X 5.1 CM

18-KARAT GOLD/SILVER BIMETAL,

18-KARAT GOLD, OIL PAINT; FABRICATED

Photo by Hap Sakwa

Each one of my jewelry pieces is a visual haiku, a way for me to capture in metal the fragility of a particular moment as I experienced it. The most important thing for me is to maintain the purity of expression in the final prize, so that the initial impetus for making it still remains alive in the end.
— MARGUERITE CHIANG

FRANCIS WILLEMSTIJN

JEREPHAES, 2003

6 x 5 x 3 CM

SILVER, COTTON, BRASS; SOLDERED, SEWN

Photo by Tessa Kleinmann

*F*rom childhood, mid-20th century typography and science fiction illustration has had a profound effect on my visual language. The bold use of line, color, and dramatic metaphor translate into my pieces, which I think of as three-dimensional illustrations. Science fiction has the power to challenge and entertain us by creating complex worlds and characters whose strangeness helps bring our own world into focus.   — MARK ROOKER

MARK ROOKER

PLAYED OUT, 1998

5.7 X 8.9 X 3.8 CM

STERLING SILVER, EBONY, ALUMINUM, AMETHYST, COPPER, NICKEL, PATINA; CARVED, FABRICATED, PLATED, ELECTROFORMED

Photos by artist

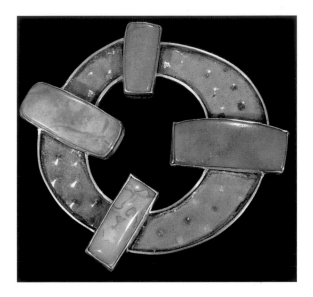

SANDRA ZILKER

INTERRUPTED DONUT, 2003

1 X 8.9 CM IN DIAMETER

STERLING SILVER, ENAMEL, COPPER, LEMON OPAL,

RHODORITE, CHRYSOPRASE, CARICITE;

TORCH FIRED, FABRICATED

Photo by Jack B. Zilker

CLAUDE SCHMITZ

FALLEN DAISY LEAVES, 2002

1.4 x 10 x 9.8 CM

18-KARAT YELLOW GOLD; SOLDERED

Photo by Christian Mosar

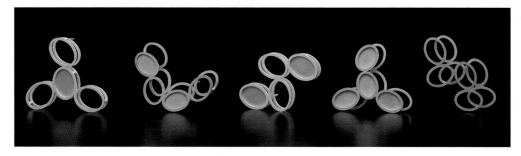

YOON JEONG KIM

FOLIAGE, 2002

LARGEST, 4.5 x 3 x 0.5 CM

STERLING SILVER, 18-KARAT GOLD; FABRICATED

Photo by Myung-Wook Huh (Studio Munch)

Every day I look at the trees, leaves, flowers, and sky and feel the wind. In the middle of the forest, there are fallen leaves, swinging on the ground, and small flowers between the rocks. They make beautiful harmony in nature. They are little things, but those small, natural elements give me fresh and vivid ideas. My imagery in jewelry comes from these natural shapes. — YOON JEONG KIM

SALLY MARSLAND

ALMOST BLACK BROOCHES, 2001–2003

3.5 TO 11.5 CM

STERLING SILVER, KING WILLIAM PINE,

INK, PAULONIA (CHINESE WOOD),

TEXTILE DYE, POLYESTER RESIN, GRAPHITE,

EPOXY RESIN, SLATE, BONE; OXIDIZED

Photos by artist

REBECCA HANNON

Lost Loves, 2003

Average, 2.5 x 2.5 x 0.6 cm

Copper, silver, patina; stamped, engraved

Photo by artist

MAH RANA

OUT OF THE DARK, 2001–2002

LARGEST, 4.8 CM

GOLD, FABRIC, PIGMENT, OIL PAINT

Photo by artist

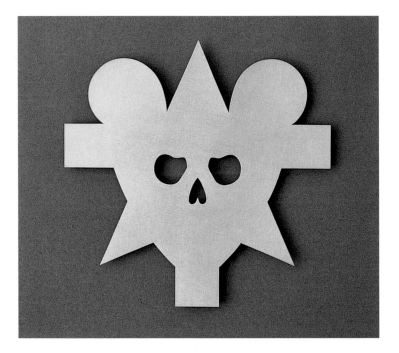

OTTO KÜNZLI

OH, SAY!, 1991

9 X 9 X 0.6 CM

GOLD

Photo by artist

JAN WEHRENS

BROOCH, 2000

7.5 x 10 x 2 CM

SILVER, PATINA

Photo by artist

THOMAS HERMAN

MONET'S DREAM, 2001

6.4 x 6.4 x 0.8 CM

BOULDER OPAL, PEARLS, 18-KARAT GOLD, LOTUS, CATTAILS;

CAST, CONSTRUCTED, CARVED, CHASED, PIERCED

Photo by Ralph Gabriner

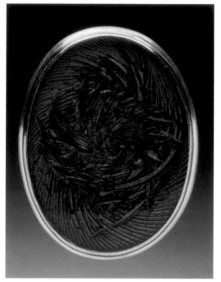

BETTINA SPECKNER

BROOCH, 2000

7.6 X 5 X 0.3 CM

ZINC, 18-KARAT GOLD, STERLING SILVER,
TURQUOISE; PHOTOETCHED

Photo by artist

Courtesy of Sienna Gallery,
Lenox, Massachusetts

JENNIFER TRASK

PAVO SWORD BROOCH, 2001

3.8 X 2.1 X 0.6 CM

STERLING SILVER, 18-KARAT GREEN
GOLD, FEATHER, LENS; FABRICATED,
CONSTRUCTED

Photo by Dean Powell

DAVID BIELANDER

PINK SNAIL, 2001

11 CM

SNAIL SHELL, RUBBER GLOVE, 18-KARAT GOLD

Photo by artist

ARIANE HARTMANN

THE BEST PLACE—COME ON EILEEN, 2003

7 X 4 X 0.2 CM

VINYL, STERLING SILVER

Photo by artist

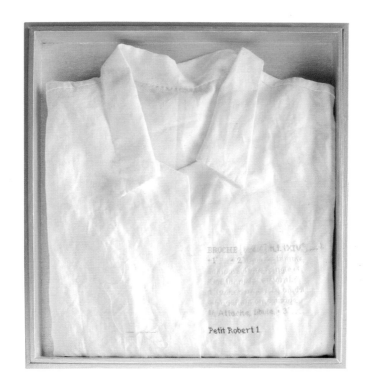

MONIKA BRUGGER

INSEPARABLE, 2002

34.2 X 31.2 X 3 CM

LINEN, SILK THREAD, WOOD

Photo by artist

DANIEL KRUGER

UNTITLED, 2003

7 x 7 x 2.5 CM

STERLING SILVER, GASPEITE FRAGMENTS, GLASS BEADS, SILK;

CHASED, KNOTTED

Photos by Nikolaus Brade

Ruudt Peters

Azoth 6 Pyrit, 2004

Largest, 3.8 x 4.2 x 3.4 cm

Silver, polyester

Photo by Rob Versluys

BEATE KLOCKMANN

UNTITLED, 2001

3.5 X 5 X 2.5 CM

GOLD; HAMMERED

Photo by artist

STEFANO MARCHETTI

BROOCH, 2001

5 X 5 X 5 CM

22-KARAT RED GOLD, 14-KARAT YELLOW GOLD

Photo by Roberto Sordi

JUDITH HOYT

RED EYEBROW, 2004

8.6 x 5 x 0.3 CM

FOUND METAL, COPPER, STAINLESS STEEL;
RIVETED, HAND-FABRICATED

Photo by John Lenz

PETRA ZIMMERMANN

PIN-UP VI, 2004

13 x 8 x 1.5 CM

DENTAL PLASTIC, STRASS (GLASS PASTE
GEMS), PYRITE, ONYX, GOLD LEAF,
SILVER; OXIDIZED

Photo by artist

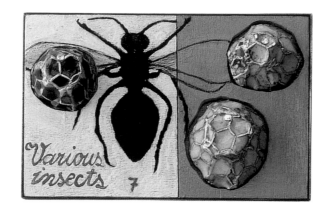

KATHLEEN FINK

UNTITLED, 2003

5 X 7.5 CM

SILVER, ENAMEL, WOOD; PAINTED

Photo by Helga Schulze-Brinkop

MARY HICKLIN AND HEATHER TRIMLETT

ANEMONE VESSEL PIN, 1992

10.2 x 7.6 x 1.9 cm

GLASS, SEED BEADS, STERLING SILVER;

HOLLOW FORMED

Photo by Melinda Holden

JIN-HEE JUNG

WHISPERING BROOCH III, IV, V, 2003

LEFT, 11 X 11 X 3.5 CM; CENTER, 12.5 X 8.5 X 4 CM;

RIGHT, 13.5 X 9.5 X 4 CM

SILVER, COPPER

Photo by Myung-Wook Huh (Studio Munch)

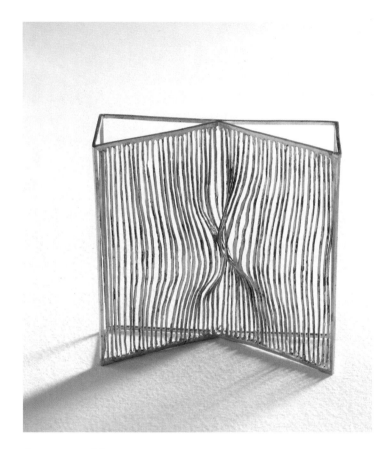

STEFANO MARCHETTI

BROOCH, 2000

6 X 5.5 X 1.5 CM

18-KARAT YELLOW GOLD

Photo by Roberto Sordi

CAROL-LYNN SWOL

UNTITLED, 2003

7.6 X 5 X 5 CM

STERLING SILVER, STEEL, TYVEK®; DYED, STACKED

Photo by artist

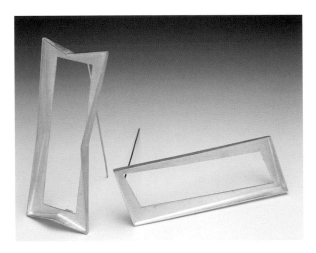

ELIZABETH BONE

BROOCHES, 1998

LEFT, 3 X 8 CM; RIGHT, 2.8 X 7.3 CM

SILVER, STEEL; FABRICATED

Photo by Joël Degen

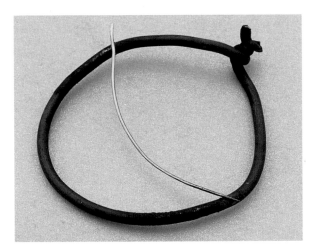

EMANUELA ZAIETTA

UNTITLED, 2003

5 X 5 CM

FOUND IRON, 18-KARAT GOLD

Photo by Federico Cavicchioli

VRATISLAV KAREL NOVÁK

STRUCTURE OF MINERAL, 1995

12 x 12 x 12 CM

STAINLESS STEEL, TIN, BRASS

Photo by Martin Tůma

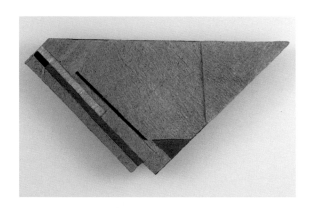

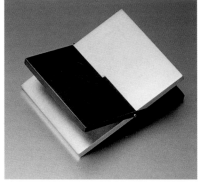

DOROTHEA HOSOM

UNTITLED, 2003

4.4 X 7.6 X 0.3 CM

TOILET PAPER, RED & BLACK MAGAZINE PAPER, FIBERBOARD, 14-KARAT GOLD FOIL; FOLDED, GLUED

Photo by artist

JI-HEE HONG

HARMONY, 2004

1.8 X 4.5 X 5.5 CM

STERLING SILVER, BOLT

Photo by Kwang-Choon Park

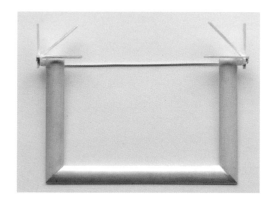

Anton Cepka

Brooch, 2003

5 x 7.5 x 1.5 cm

Silver; soldered

Photo by Matúš Cepka

SALLY MARSLAND

SOME BROOCHES THAT ARE ROUND, 1997

0.8 TO 7.5 CM IN DIAMETER

STERLING SILVER, ANODIZED ALUMINUM;

CAST, LATHE-TURNED

Photo by artist

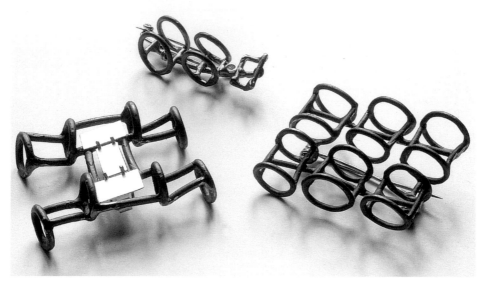

ANTJE BRAEUER

VEHICLES, 2002

AVERAGE, 1 X 6 X 4 CM

TITANIUM, IRON, GOLD; CAST

Photo by Helga Schulze-Brinkop

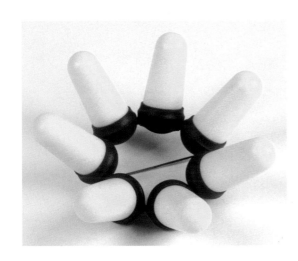

JIRO KAMATA

TSUBOMI, 2003

6 X 6 X 3 CM

EAR PLUGS, SILVER; OXIDIZED

Photos by artist

HELEN BRITTON

PINK GARDEN, 2003

4 x 3 x 3 CM

PAINT, SILVER

Photo by artist

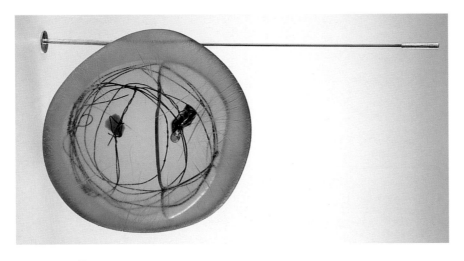

MARZIA ROSSI

ICE, 2002

5 X 4.5 X 0.9 CM

THERMOPLASTIC, SILVER, GLASS, OIL

Photo by Federico Cavicchioli

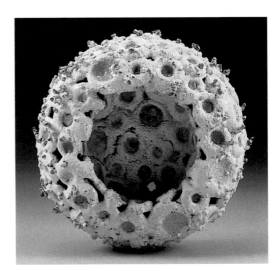

HYE-YOUNG SUH

*BGE*13*, 2003

7.6 X 7.6 X 2.5 CM

ENAMEL, COPPER, STERLING SILVER;

ELECTROFORMED

Photo by artist

KADRI MÄLK

EVERY ANGEL IS TERRIBLE, 2001

7.2 X 6 X 2.1 CM

WHITE GOLD, JET, SEPIA, BLACK CORAL, HYACINTH

Photo by Tiit Rammul

IDA LINDBERG

UNTITLED, 2003

8 X 8 X 0.2 CM

SILVER, FABRIC

Photo by artist

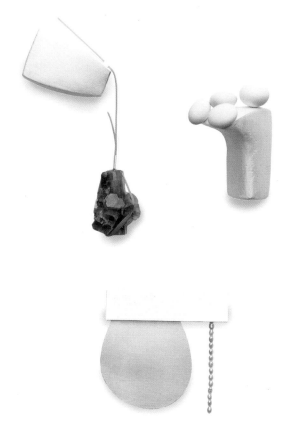

IRIS BODEMER

UNTITLED, 1999

LARGEST, 11 X 6 X 2 CM

SILVER, ARAGONITE, PLASTIC, PEBBLES, PEARLS

Photo by Julian Kirschler

Sybille Richter

Ansteckschmuck, 2003

4 x 8.5 x 6 cm

Sterling silver, polyester resin; cast

Photo by artist

SABINE STEINHÄUSLER

NESTBROSCHEN (NEST BROOCHES), 2002

LEFT, 1.9 X 4.1 X 3.1 CM; CENTER, 1.8 X 2.9 X 3.3 CM;

RIGHT, 1.7 X 4.8 X 3.1 CM

SILVER, BRASS, PATINA

Photo by Paul Müller

KAYO SAITO

RUSTLING BROOCH, 2003

EACH, 5 X 10 X 3 CM

SILVER, MAGNETS

Photo by artist

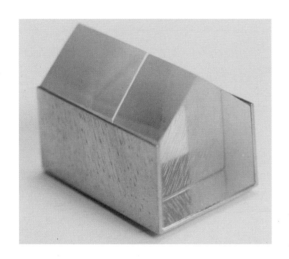

MARIA VALDMA

…WHEN THE RAIN CAME

THROUGH THE ROOF, 2002

2 x 2 x 2.5 CM

GOLD, SILVER, THERMOPLASTIC; PLATED

Photo by Mihkel Valdma

ABRASHA

SQUARE PIN #12, 1990

5 x 5 x 1.4 CM

STERLING SILVER, STEEL NAILS,

STAINLESS STEEL; FABRICATED

Photo by artist

KATHLEEN FINK

UNTITLED, 2003

10 X 12 CM

SILVER; NIELLO, GRANULATED

Photo by Helga Schulze-Brinkop

CHARLOTTA NORRMAN

MY BIG BROTHER, 2001

20 X 30 X 5 CM

PHOTOGRAPH, MEDIUM-DENSITY FIBERBOARD, SILVER

Photo by artist

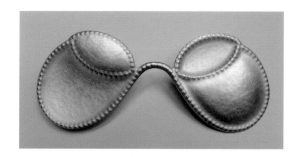

BIRGIT LAKEN

SEED VESSEL, 2003

4 X 9 X 0.3 CM

SILVER; PRESSED, HAMMERED

Photo by artist

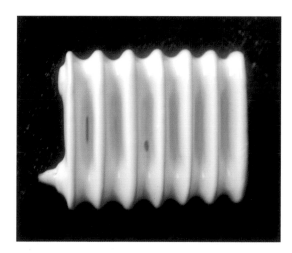

MIRJAM NORINDER

RADIATOR, 2004

3.5 X 4.5 X 1 CM

SILVER, WOOD, LACQUER

Photo by artist

SUZANNE ESSER

UNTITLED, 2001

EACH, 18 X 17 X 1.7 CM

EBONY; LATHE-SCULPTED, PAINTED

Photo by Ron Zijlstra

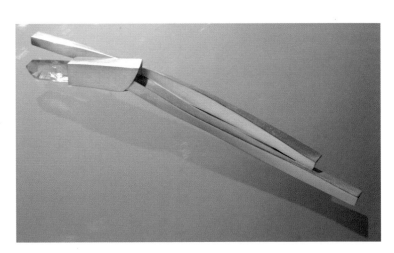

YVONNE GALLEY-KNAPPE

UNTITLED, 2003

13 X 2 X 1 CM

SILVER, ROCK CRYSTAL

Photo by Christoph Petras

This brooch was inspired by the lava-covered landscape. The mirror underneath reflects light through the cracks of the black sheet above, suggesting life and movement underneath the surface. — YOKO SHIMIZU

YOKO SHIMIZU

LAVA, 2003

1.5 x 12 x 3.5 CM

SILVER, MIRROR; NIELLO

Photo by Federico Cavacchioli

T̲he stamp is a translation of the labels tagged on clothing, but in this case adapted to the human body. This stamp decorates the body as a tattoo and provides information, the ingredients about the human body, which could be related to jewelry and clothing. Instead of decorating your clothes with a brooch, you have to find a special place on your own body to decorate.

— CATHELIJNE ENGELKES

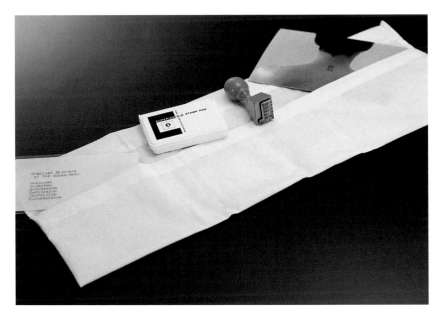

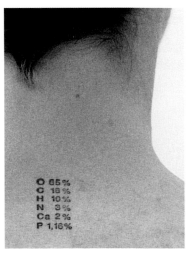

CATHELIJNE ENGELKES

THE CHEMICAL ELEMENTS OF A HUMAN BODY, 2003

STAMP, 2.6 X 1.7 CM; DISPLAY, 20 X 54 CM

STAMP, PHOTO INDICATION, INK, TEXTILE, SEALED PAPER

Photo by Craft Center, Itamy City, Japan

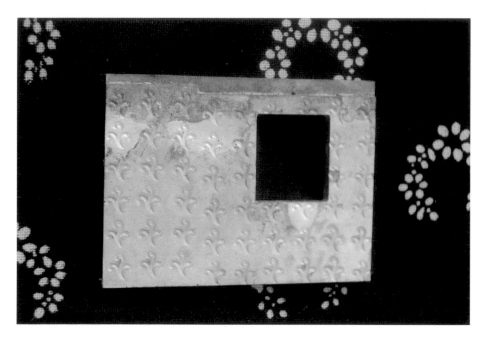

MIRJAM NORINDER

WALLPAPER, 2004

5 X 4 CM

SILVER; SOLDERED

Photo by artist

KADRI MÄLK

MEDUSA, 2004

9 X 6 X 2.4 CM

OXIDIZED SILVER, RUBBER

Photo by Tiit Rammul

DANIEL KRUGER

UNTITLED, 2004

7.5 X 7.5 X 3 CM

COPPER, SILK, 18-KARAT GOLD;

CHASED, FORGED, KNOTTED

Photo by Nikolaus Brade

JOHN KENT GARROTT

IGNITION BROOCH, 2003

5 X 7.6 X 5 CM

STERLING SILVER, IGNITED ALCOHOL

Photo by artist

RAÏSSA BUMP

BROOCH, 2003

4.1 X 3.8 X 0.3 CM

STERLING SILVER, ENAMEL, ROUGH DIAMONDS,

18-KARAT GOLD

Photo by Kevin Sprague

Courtesy of Sienna Gallery, Lenox, Massachusetts

DEBORAH ALEXANDER

FRAGMENTS OF THE PAST, 2003

3.8 X 3.8 X 0.6 CM

24-KARAT GOLD, STERLING SILVER;

DIE PRESSED, FABRICATED

Photo by Margot Geist

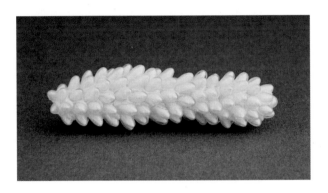

KRISTI PAAP

OBSESSION, 2003

6 x 1.5 x 1.5 CM

THERMOPLASTIC, PIGMENT, SILVER

Photo by Mihkel Valdma

BIRGIT LAKEN

ANTIQUITY, 2001–2002

4 x 4 x 0.4 CM

FRESHWATER PEARLS, NYLON, SILVER;

HAMMERED, CONSTRUCTED

Photo by artist

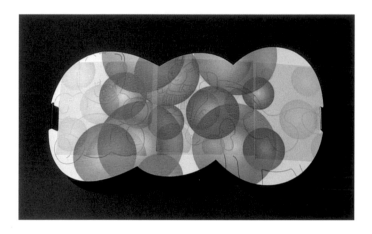

NORMAN WEBER

HAUS & GARTEN #18 (HOUSE & GARDEN #18), 2003

6.3 X 12.4 X 2.1 CM

SILVER, STEEL, C-PRINT

Photo by artist

PETRA ZIMMERMANN

UNTITLED, 2003

11.5 X 7.2 X 0.7 CM

SILVER; NIELLO, OXIDIZED

Photo by artist

MARK ROOKER

REGULAR PROGRAMMING, 2000

EACH, 15.2 x 6.4 x 3.2 CM

STERLING SILVER, NIOBIUM, BRASS, COPPER, GOLD, ALUMINUM, ACRYLIC, GEMSTONE
BEADS, PVC, PAINT, GLASS; ANODIZED, CARVED, FABRICATED, ELECTROFORMED

Photo by artist

HIROKO YAMADA

TRUFFLE TO WEAR, 2004

7.6 X 5 X 5 CM

18-KARAT GOLD, SILVER/COPPER MOKUME GANE,

YELLOW SAPPHIRE; RAISED

Photo by artist

BEATE KLOCKMANN

UNTITLED, 2001

7 X 7 X 1.5 CM

GOLD; HAMMERED

Photo by artist

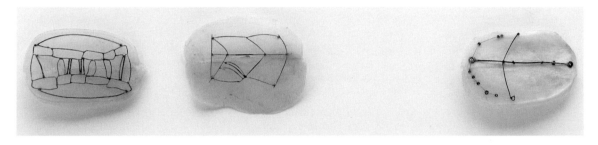

BEATE EISMANN

3 BROOCHES, 2000

EACH, 6 X 9 X 0.3 CM

SHRIMP CRACKERS, SILVER, NICKEL SILVER, STEEL WIRE

Photo by Helga Schulze-Brinkop

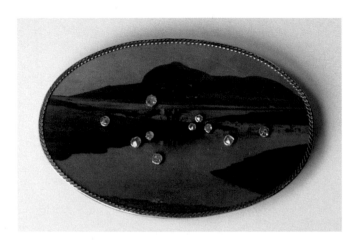

BETTINA SPECKNER

UNTITLED, 2003

4 X 6 CM

ZINC, SILVER, DIAMONDS;
PHOTOETCHED

Photo by artist

ALESSIA SEMERARO

ALTARE BIANCO, 2003

5 X 9 X 0.5 CM

RECYCLED IRON, GOLD, SILVER;
PIERCED, SOLDERED

Photo by artist

BIC TIEU

SEASON SERIES BROOCHES, 2003

EACH, 3.5 X 3.8 X 0.6 CM

STERLING SILVER, VENEER PLYWOOD, STAINLESS

STEEL, ENAMEL; FORGED, LASER ENGRAVED

Photo by artist

KARIN SEUFERT

UNTITLED, 1995

5.7 X 1.6 X 1 CM

SODA CAN, REMANIUM;

CUT, SLIT, FOLDED

Photo by artist

RENEE BEVAN

UNTITLED, 2002

LARGEST, 5 X 2.5 X 6 CM

SILVER, STAINLESS STEEL WIRE, RESIN, FABRIC, WAX,

LATEX, SPONGE, CHERRY STALKS; POWDER COATED

Photos by artist

YOKO SHIMIZU

FROZEN, 2002

6 X 6 X 1.5 CM

PAPER, RESIN, SILVER

Photo by Federico Cavacchioli

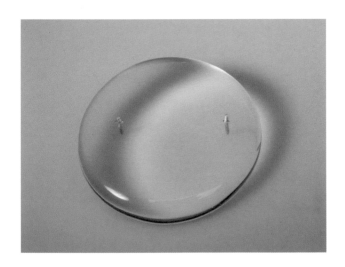

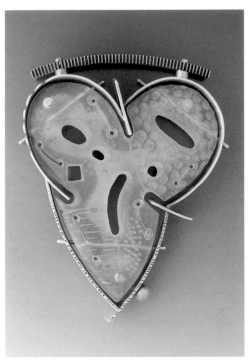

PAVEL HERYNEK

WATER II, 2002

1.5 x 6.3 CM IN DIAMETER

THERMOPLASTIC, STAINLESS STEEL

Photo by Markéta Ondrusková

THOMAS MANN

FLOAT SERIES—ANIMATED HEART, 2004

8.9 x 6.4 CM

SILVER, ACRYLIC, BRASS, BRONZE

Photo by Angele Seiley for Thomas Mann Design

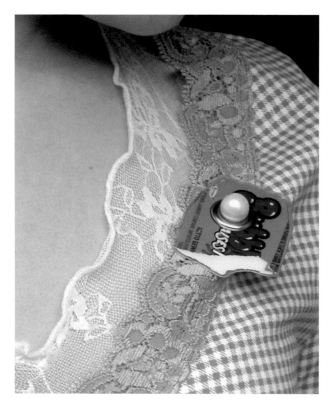
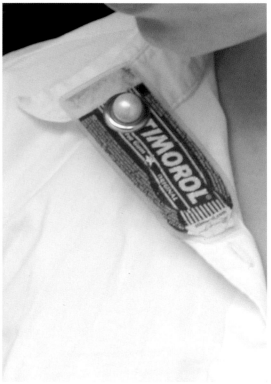

MECKY VAN DEN BRINK

GUM ADDICTION, 2002

CANDY WRAPPER, 8.5 X 3.5 X 1 CM;

PINK BUBBLE, 5.5 X 4 X 1 CM

PAPER, PLASTIC, METAL, PEARL

Photos by artist

M O N I K A B R U G G E R

SEWN WITH RED THREAD, 2003

34.4 X 31.2 X 3 CM

COTTON CHEMISE, THIMBLE, SILVER,

SILK THREAD, GOLD NEEDLE, WOOD

Photo by artist

STELLAN ERIKZÉN HERMOND

SUPERHJÄLTEKNAPP (SUPERHERO BUTTON), 2004

3.5 X 3.5 X 1.8 CM

SILVER, ACRYLIC, DIODE, MICROSWITCH, BATTERY

Photos by artist

ANNAMARIA ZANELLA

BLUE CELL, 2003

8 x 5.5 x 1.8 CM

PAPIER–MÂCHÉ, GOLD, PAINT, WAX

Photo by Ferdinand Neumüller

RUUDT PETERS

AZOTH 3B QUARZ, 2004

6 X 4.7 X 1.5 CM

SILVER, POLYESTER

Photo by Rob Versluys

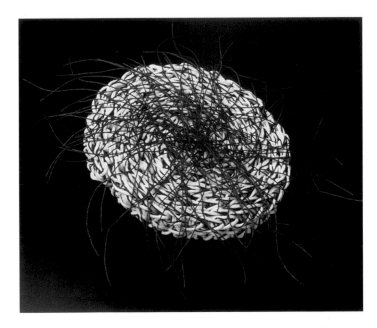

SUSAN CROSS

CONCENTRATION, 2001

6.5 CM IN DIAMETER

PAPER CORD, COTTON THREAD; SPUN, CROCHETED

Photo by Joël Degen

BRUNE BOYER-PELLEREJ

CHEMINEZ BROOCH, 2003

9.5 X 4 CM

FINE GOLD, IRON

Photo by Michel Azous

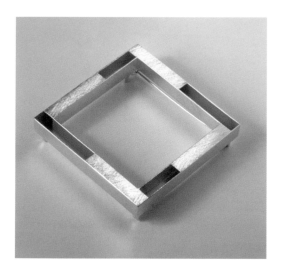

MICHAEL BECKER

Brooch, 2003

5 x 5 cm

18-KARAT GOLD; FABRICATED

Photo by Walter Maberland

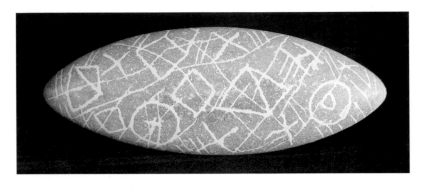

ANDREW GOSS

GEOMETRY, 2003

2.3 X 6 X 0.5 CM

CONCRETE, CEMENT; CAST, SCRIBED, CEMENT-FILLED

Photo by artist

MYOUNG SUN LEE

PSYCHOLOGICAL DISTANCE 1, 2003

5.5 X 6.5 X 0.5 CM

IRON, SILVER

Photo by Myung-Wook Huh (Studio Munch)

RIAN DE JONG

AUTUMN, 2002

2.5 x 11 x 0.5 CM

BLACK CORAL, RED CORAL, SILVER; ASSEMBLED

Photo by artist

KATJA PRINS

UNTITLED, 2003

10 x 12 x 8 CM

ALPACA, SEALING WAX

Photo by Eddo Hartmann

PAOLO MARCOLONGO

CONVERSATION WITH ARCHITECTURE, 2003

2.7 X 2.2 X 1.3 CM

STERLING SILVER, GLASS

Photos by Giustino Chemello

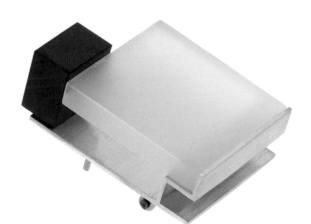

PAOLO MARCOLONGO

CONVERSATION WITH ARCHITECTURE, 2003

2.7 X 2.4 X 1.2 CM

STERLING SILVER, QUARTZ, GLASS

Photo by Giustino Chemello

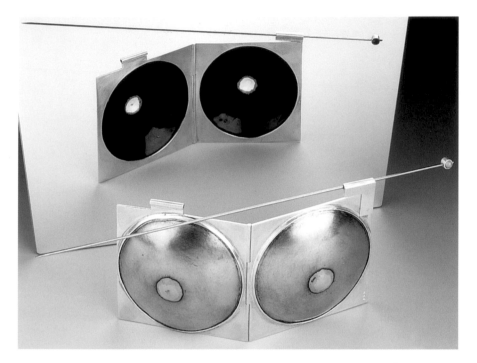

LUDMILA ŠIKOLOVÁ

BROOCH, FROM THE SERIES *JEWELRY FOR PAVEL*, 1995

6.5 x 13 x 0.2 CM

SILVER, COPPER, ENAMEL

Photo by Martin Tůma

FELIEKE VAN DER LEEST

TREE FROG WITH KNICKERBOCKERS, 2003

11.5 x 8 x 3 CM

TEXTILE, RUBBER, GOLD, STORE-BOUGHT TOY;

CROCHETED, FORGED

Photo by Eddo Hartmann

PIERRE CAVALAN

VICTORIA CROSS MEDAL FOR A NEW DAY, 2002–2003

9.5 X 9.5 X 1.3 CM

FOUND OBJECTS; ASSEMBLED

Photo by Julian Wolkenstein

BRIDGET CATCHPOLE

SHORT AND CURLY, 2002

3.2 X 1.9 X 1.9 CM

STERLING SILVER, SYNTHETIC BRISTLES; CONSTRUCTED

Photo by Anthony McLean

PETRA MANDAL

UNTITLED, 2001

5 X 10.5 X 7 CM

BOOKMARK, MODELING CLAY, PAPIER-MÂCHÉ

Photo by artist

IRIS BODEMER

UNTITLED, 1998

7.5 X 11 X 1.5 CM

18-KARAT GOLD, DRAGON PEARL, RUBBER, TAPE,

RECONSTRUCTED IVORY

Photo by Julian Kirschler

PETRA ZIMMERMAN

EVEREST, 2003

8.3 x 11.2 x 3.2 cm

SILVER, DENTAL PLASTIC, ROCK CRYSTAL, SILVER LEAF

Photo by Kevin Sprague

Courtesy of Sienna Gallery, Lenox, Massachusetts

This brooch was inspired by a drawing of a drain cover by Joseph Beuys. I made it in memory of my parents, who had both recently passed away, four months apart from each other. In it I used Gematria, a Kabbalistic numbers game often used to explain or make connections between words, phrases, and/or entire passages of the Torah, Talmud, etc. The basis for this discipline is that every letter of the Hebrew alphabet has a certain numerical value; thus, words have a numerical value. The Hebrew word meaning "life" has a numerical value of 18. The brooch has 36 hollow rivets. 36 = 2 x 18, representing the lives of both my parents. The rivets are both visual and functional. They hold the back plate with the closing mechanism against the drain cover. — ABRASHA

ABRASHA
DRAIN COVER BROOCH, 1996
7.9 X 0.9 CM
ALUMINUM, STERLING SILVER,
24-KARAT GOLD, STAINLESS STEEL;
FABRICATED, RIVETED
Photo by artist

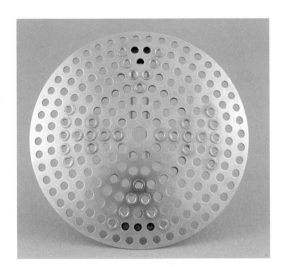

SYBILLE RICHTER

ANSTECKSCHMUCK, 2002

3 X 8.5 X 6 CM

STERLING SILVER, POLYESTER RESIN, CORD; CAST

Photo by artist

GRAZIANO VISINTIN

UNTITLED, 1982

10 X 2 CM

18–KARAT YELLOW GOLD,

18–KARAT WHITE GOLD

Photo by Lorenzo Trento

MARZIA ROSSI

ICE, 2002

5 X 4.5 X 1.4 CM

THERMOPLASTIC, SILVER, GLASS

Photo by Federico Cavicchioli

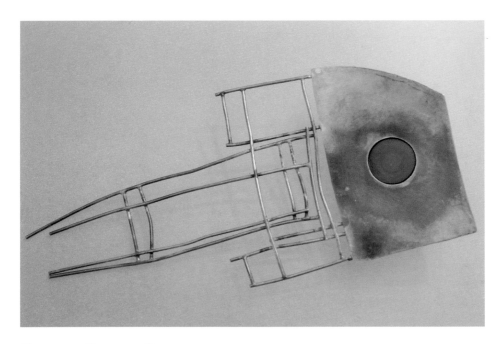

YVONNE GALLEY-KNAPPE

BLUE SECRET, 2000

10 X 4.5 X 0.5 CM

SILVER, GLASS

Photo by Christoph Petras

RIAN DE JONG

CONTAINER, 2002

4 X 4 X 2.5 CM

BLACK CORAL, MODEL–MAKING

PLASTIC, ARTIFICIAL HAIR,

SILVER; ASSEMBLED

Photo by artist

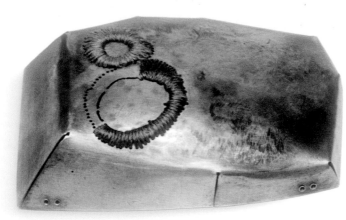

SYBILLE RICHTER

ANSTECKSCHMUCK, 2003

2 X 8 X 6 CM

STERLING SILVER, CORD

Photo by artist

HIROKO YAMADA

TRUFFLE OF THE DAY TO WEAR, 2004

6.4 x 15.2 x 22.9 CM

OBSIDIAN, QUARTZ, RUBY, 18-KARAT GOLD, SILVER/COPPER MOKUME
GANE, YELLOW SAPPHIRE; HAND-CUT, POLISHED, RAISED

Photo by artist

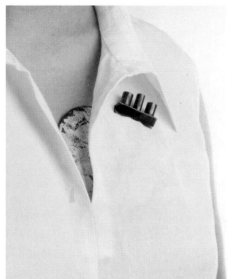

BRUNE BOYER-PELLEREJ

CHEMINEZ BROOCH, 1999

11.5 x 10 CM

COPPER, GOLD LEAF, IRON

Photos by Michel Azous

YEONMI KANG

SELF-PORTRAIT, 2003

7.3 X 5.7 X 2.5 CM

STERLING SILVER, ENAMEL, 18-KARAT GOLD,

24-KARAT GOLD LEAF; CAST, FABRICATED, KUM BOO

Photo by Yongwha Kang

JAMIE BENNETT

LUMEN #9, 2002

4.7 X 5 X 0.6 CM

ENAMEL, 18-KARAT GOLD

Photo by Kevin Sprague

Courtesy of Sienna Gallery,

Lenox, Massachusetts

KRISTI PAAP

HONEY-SWEET, 1999

7 x 2 x 2 CM

THERMOPLASTIC,

GOLD LEAF, TOMBAC

Photo by Mihkel Valdma

BETTINA SPECKNER

UNTITLED, 2002

4.5 x 8 CM

ZINC, 18-KARAT GOLD; PHOTOETCHED

Photo by artist

SUNGHO CHO

SEA IN MY MEMORY, 2003

LEFT, 7 X 7 X 1.7 CM; CENTER, 7 X 8 X 2 CM; RIGHT, 12 X 8.5 X 2 CM

STERLING SILVER, STEEL; CAST

Photo by Myung-Wook Huh (Studio Munch)

MARIA VALDMA

NORA, 2003

6 X 4 CM

WOOD, PHOTOCOPY, SILVER; PAINTED

Photo by Mihkel Valdma

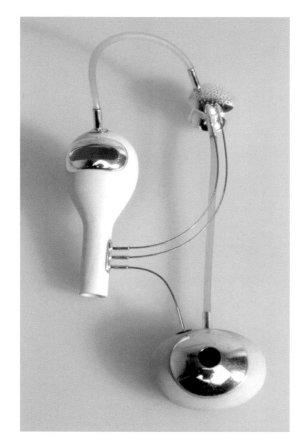

ANNIKA ÅKERFELT

UNTITLED, 2002

12 X 7 X 2 CM

PORCELAIN, SILVER, RUBBER, WIRE

Photo by artist

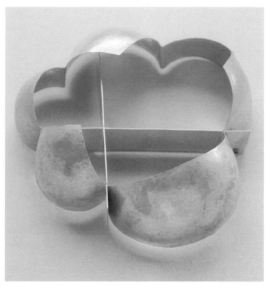

MINDY HERRIN

SIMONE & BELLA, 2002

8.9 X 3.8 X 1.9 CM

SILVER; FABRICATED

Photo by artist

BEATE KLOCKMANN

UNTITLED, 2001

7 X 7 X 2.5 CM

GOLD; HAMMERED

Photo by artist

ARTIST INDEX

ACKNOWLEDGMENTS

I would like to thank editor Marthe Le Van for the opportunity to participate in this project. Marthe and her capable assistant Nathalie Mornu made a challenging jury situation as pleasant as they possibly could for me and my colleague Biba Schutz. Although I take full responsibility for the final selection, I am most grateful for Biba's contributions throughout the jurying process. Her critical eye and her judgment, without regard to her personal taste, made her an invaluable partner. It goes without saying that my deepest gratitude goes to the many artists who have trusted me with their stories and allowed me to represent them.

Marjorie Simon

ABOUT THE JUROR

Marjorie Simon is a studio jeweler who also teaches and writes about craft. She is chairperson of the Editorial Advisory Committee for *Metalsmith* and writes regularly for the magazine. She has written essays for international catalogues, and she curated *The EnvironMental Bead*, a traveling exhibition. In 1995 she began enameling and recently has been exploring botanical themes. She has received two fellowships from the New Jersey State Council on the Arts.

MARK ROOKER *REGULAR PROGRAMMING*, 2000